Frederick St. George de Lautour Booth-Tucker

One hundred favorite songs and music of the Salvation Army

Together with a collection of fifty songs and solos. Second Edition

Frederick St. George de Lautour Booth-Tucker

One hundred favorite songs and music of the Salvation Army
Together with a collection of fifty songs and solos. Second Edition

ISBN/EAN: 9783337266219

Printed in Europe, USA, Canada, Australia, Japan

Cover: Foto ©Thomas Meinert / pixelio.de

More available books at **www.hansebooks.com**

ONE HUNDRED

Favorite Songs and Music

OF

THE SALVATION ARMY

TOGETHER WITH A COLLECTION OF FIFTY
SONGS AND SOLOS

SECOND  EDITION

COMPILED BY

COMMANDER BOOTH TUCKER

Price:
Board, 25 cents; $18 per hundred.
Cloth, 50 cents.

NEW YORK CITY:
THE SALVATION ARMY PUBLISHING HOUSE, 120-124 WEST 14th STREET

COMMANDER BOOTH TUCKER. CONSUL BOOTH TUCKER.

PREFACE.

MUSIC voices the heart-throbs of humanity. It crystalizes the tear in the eye of sorrow, and lends wings to earth's joys, and yet too often, alas, its charms are sacrificed before the Moloch of self-interest. But never is music more beautiful, more powerful, more inspiring than when it fulfils the purpose for which it was intended—the lifting and linking of the human to the Divine. Enshrined in this casket, the Gospel message, so glorious in itself, glitters with resplendent lustre.

Many a hardened heart, which has become deaf to the appeals of conscience, and insensible even to its own everlasting interests, has awakened to new life under the magic spell of song.

Nor has The Salvation Army from its very earliest inception been oblivious to the immense value of music in connection with its far-reaching mission.

A shrewd observer prophesied many years ago that it was destined to "sing its way around the world." But even he could hardly have foreseen that its own composers and poets would soon be creating a new chapter in the history of religious music and song, and that hundreds of new melodies, together with an average of over 5,000 new hymns, would be annually poured forth in an ever-increasing Niagara of harmony.

It will thus be understood that to make a selection from the most popular of these has been no easy task, although we have confined ourselves almost entirely to the composition of our Army musicians, many of .

whose names and songs have already become famous, being translated into nearly all the leading languages of the world. Field Commissioner Miss Eva Booth, who commands in Canada, and Major Slater, of the International Headquarters, are among our principal musical contributors, while a goodly quota of American composers have added to the list.

One special feature of this present volume has been the inclusion of a number of the most popular secular airs by famous American composers. Among others we are greatly indebted to Professor Chas. K. Harris and Professor Paul Dresser for the permission they have kindly granted us to use some of their favorite melodies, for which words have been specially written by our Army song-writers. The collection will thus emphasize one of the most striking features of Salvation Army warfare, the adaptation of religious words to purely secular airs. "The Banks of the Wabash," "Just Break the News to Mother," and "Tell Her That You Saw Me," are amongst the tunes that have thus been dealt with.

In regard to songs borrowed from other sources, we have sought to obtain previous permission, when this has been necessary, and to acknowledge the sources to which we were indebted. Should we have failed in any instances we shall be glad to acknowledge our oversight in future issues. We are indebted to the following publishers and composers to use some of their songs: The John Church Company; Messrs. Howley, Haviland & Company; Messrs. Eaton & Mains; Professor Chas. K. Harris; Mr. Paul Dresser; Dr. J. E. Rankin.

A considerable number of songs without music have also been added in order to aid its use for congregational purposes.

In conclusion, we would say that the object of this book is the conversion of sinners, the sanctification of saints and the infusion of the war spirit among Salvationists and professing Christians. Nearly every song included in the list has actually accomplished definite results of the above character, and with the earnest prayer that as feathering to the arrow God may make this music to His truth, we launch our effort upon the field of humanity's need.

F. deLautour Booth Tucker

1.
From the General Down to Me.

Words and Music by W. A. HAWLEY.
Charlottetown, P. E. Island.

1 We have girded on our ar - mor, we're marching bold-ly on;
2. We... love salva-tion war-fare, to fight is our de-light.
3. O .... rebel friend sur-ren-der, lay down your pu-ny arms,

Cho—*From the Gen'-ral down to me, we're in for vic-to-ry;*

The en - e-my's de - termin'd, but the bat-tle must be won;
And when the bat-tle's o - ver here we'll wear a crown so bright;
We'll save you from your dan-ger, and from Sa-tan's art - ful charms,

We'll win the fight for God and right, on er - 'ry land and sea;

Sal - va - tion is our song, the Blood is all our plea;
Till there with shield and song, we're marching bold and free,
Come, meet our great Commander, re - ceive a par - don free,

Un - der the col-ors three, for life we mean to be,

D. C. for chorus.

We'll fight the foe where-e'er we go, from the General down to me.
And blow on blow, we'll smite the foe, from the General down to me.
We'll all shout Hal-le - lu - jah! from the General down to me.

We'll push the war that's what we're for, from the General down to me.

(5)

2. Climbing up the Golden Stair.

Words by CONSUL BOOTH TUCKER.　　　　　Music by COMMANDER BOOTH TUCKER.

1. Oh, my heart is full of mu - sic and of glad - ness,
2. Ev - 'ry day it seems I want to serve Him bet - ter,
3. Oh, the joy of get - ting oth - ers to climb with me,

As on wings of love and faith I up - ward fly, upward fly,
Ev - 'ry day it seems I want to love Him more; love Him more,
Lost, des - pair - ing, brok - en - heart - ed, all may come; all may come,

Not a shad - ow - cloud my Sav - iour's face ob - scur - ing,
Ev - 'ry day I strive to climb the lad - der fast - er,
Calv - 'ry's love has made this stair a ve - ry wide one,

As I'm climb - ing to my home-stead in the sky.
Ev - 'ry ef - fort brings me near - er Ca - naan's shore.
Sin - ner, lay your bur - den down and hast - en home.

CHORUS.

Oh, I'm climb-ing up the gold-en stair to Glo - ry, Oh, I'm

Climbing up the Golden Stair.

climbing with my golden crown be - fore me; I am climbing in the light,

I am climbing day and night, I shall shout with all my might when I get

there! Oh, I'm climbing up the gold-en stair to Glo - ry, Oh, I'm

climbing with my gold-en crown be-fore me; I am climbing in the light,

I am climbing day and night, I am climbing up the gold-en stair.

3.

Tarry at the Cross of Jesus.

Words and Music by COMMANDER H. H. BOOTH.

mf Allegro.

1. Je - sus is my Saviour, this I know, He has giv-en peace to my heart;
2. There I came to Je-sus, bound and sad, Lib- er - ty I claim'd from my sin;
3. Would you know the peace which Jesus gives? Would you know the joy He bestows?

When my soul was burden'd, fill'd full of woe, Seeking from my sin to part,
Read - i - ly He gave it, and, oh, so glad Was my heart then made by Him!
Would you know the strength the sinner re-ceives When his heart the blood o'erflows?

cres.

Graciously He heard me when I pray'd, Drew me to His riv - en side,
Fetters which had bound me He destroyed, Bless-ed is the spot to me
Comrade, come along then, let us go Where the precious fountain springs,

f

There by faith I wash'd, and so was sav'd, His Blood was there ap - plied.
Where I knelt to thank Him, o - ver-joyed To find my soul was free!
That can make the sin - ner white as snow, Re- mov - ing all his sins

f CHORUS.

Oh, that's the place where I love to be, For mighty wonders there I see,

Tarry at the Cross of Jesus.

cres. *ff*

Would you be blest, then tar - ry with me At the Cross of Je - sus.

4. Blessed Jesus, Save our Children.

Words by CONSUL BOOTH-TUCKER.

1. { Bless-ed Je-sus, save our children! Be their guardian thro' life's way; }
   { From all evil e'er protect them, Walk Thou with them, come what may, }

2. { Bless-ed Je-sus, lead our children In - to paths of ser-vice sweet, }
   { Up the hill of Calvary climb-ing, May they and the sin-ner meet! }

3. { Bless-ed Je-sus, make our chil-dren Thine for life and Thine for aye! }
   { When death's waters overtake them, Be their Rock, their Light, their Stay! }

In white rai-ment Let us meet them, When earth's shadows flee a - way;
More than conquerors Let us see them Bring their jew-els to Thy feet;
Ten - der Shepherd, Let us find them On Thy breast in realms of day;

In white rai-ment Let us meet them, When earth's shadows flee a-way.
More than conquerors Let us see them Bring their jewels to Thy feet.
Tender Shepherd, Let us find them On Thy breast in realms of day.

5.

The Heavenly Gales are Blowing.

Words by GENERAL BOOTH.

mf *Moderato.*

1. Oh, boundless Sal - va - tion! deep o - cean of love! Oh, full-ness of
2. My sins they are man - y, their stains are so deep, And bit - ter the
3. Oh, o - cean of mer - cy, oft long- ing I've stood, On the brink of Thy
4. The tide now is flow - ing, I'm touch - ing the wave, I hear the loud
5. And now, hal - le - lu - jah! the rest of my days, Shall glad - ly be

mer - cy Christ brought from a-bove, The whole world re - deem-ing, so
tears of re - morse that I weep; But use - less is weep - ing, Thou
won - der - ful life - giv - ing flood; Once more I have reached this
call of "The might - y to save," My faith's grow-ing bold - er de -
spent in pro - mot - ing His praise; Who o - pened His bo - som to

mf   *cres.*

rich and so free, Now flow - ing for all men, now flow - ing for
great crim-son sea, Thy wa - ters can cleanse me, Thy wa - ters can
soul - clean-ing sea, I will not go back, I will not go
liv - ered I'll be,— I plunge 'neath the wa - ters, I plunge 'neath the
pour out this sea Of bound-less sal - va - tion, Of bound-less sal -

f

all men, Now flow - ing for all men, come, roll o - ver me.
cleanse me, Thy wa - ters can cleanse me, come, roll o - ver me.
back, I will not go back till it rolls o - ver me.
wa - ters, I plunge 'neath the wa - ters—they roll o - ver me.
va - tion, Of bound-less sal - va - tion for you and for me.

The Heavenly Gales are Blowing.

f CHORUS. *Allegretto.*

The heav'n-ly gales are blow-ing, The cleansing sea is flow-ing, Be-neath its waves I'm go-ing, Hal-le-lu-jah! praise the Lord!

Chorus.

Words and Music by J. OXLEY.

He from thy bur-den will give re-lief, He from thy sor-row will give re-lease, For Je-sus knows all thy heart's deep grief, He's wait-ing to wel-come thee home.....

(11)

6.

The Penitent's Plea.

Words and Music by COMMANDER H. H. BOOTH

Andante con espress.

1. Sav - iour, hear me, while be-fore Thy feet   I   the rec-ord of my
Canst   Thou still in mer - cy think   of   me.   Stoop   to set my shackled

sins re - peat,   Stained with guilt, myself ab-hor - ing.
spir - it free,

Filled with grief, my soul out-pour - ing;   Raise my sinking heart, and

but me   be   Thy   child   once   more!

(12)

The Penitent's Plea.

CHORUS.

Grace there is my ev'ry debt to pay, Blood to wash my ev'ry sin a-way, Pow'r to keep me spot-less day by day, For me, for me!

2 All the memories of deeds gone by
Rise within me and Thy pow'r defy;
With a deathly chill ensnaring,
They would leave my soul desparing.
Saviour, take my hand, I cannot tell
How to stem the tides that round me
swell,
How to ease my conscience, or to quell
My flaming heart.

3 Back with all the guilt my spirit bears,
Past the haunting memories of years,
Self and shame and fear despising,
Foes and taunting fiends surprising;
Saviour, to Thy Cross I press my way,
And a broken heart before it lay;
Ere I leave, oh, let me hear Thee say,
"I will be Thine."

4 Yet why should I fear, hast Thou not
died
That no seeking soul should be denied?
To that heart its sins confessing,
Canst Thou fail to give a blessing?
By the love and pity Thou hast shown,
By the blood that did for me atone,
Boldly will I kneel before Thy throne,
A pleading soul.

5 All the rivers of Thy grace I claim,
Over ev'ry promise write my name;
As I am I come believing,
As Thou art Thou dost, receiving,
Bid me rise a freed and pardoned slave;
Master o'er my sin, the world, the grave,
Charging me to preach Thy power to
To sin-bound souls.   [save,

(13)

7. Victory for Me.

Words and Music by COMMANDER HERBERT BOOTH.

mf Allegro

1. To the front! the cry is ring - ing, To the front! your place is
2. To the front! the fight is rag - ing, Christ's own banner leads the
3. To the front! no more de-lay - ing, Wound - ed spir-its need thy

there, In the conflict men are want - ed, Men of
way, Ev - 'ry pow'r and tho't en-gag - ing, Might di-
care: To the front! thy Lord o-bey - ing, Stoop to

dim.

hope, and faith, and pray'r; . . . . Self - ish ends shall claim no right
vine shall be our stay; . . . . . We have heard the cry for help.
help the dy - ing there: . . . . . Brok-en hearts and blighted hopes,

From the bat - tle's post to take us, Fear shall van - ish
From the dy - ing mil - lions round us, We've re-ceived the
Slaves of sin and de - gra - da - tion, Wait for thee, in

Victory for Me.

in   the fight,   For   tri-umph-ant God will   make   us.
royal   com-mand   From   our dy-ing Lord who   found   us.
love   to bring   Ho - ly peace and lib-er - a - tion.

ff Chorus.

No re - treat-ing, Hell de - feat - ing, Shoul-der   to shoul - der we

stand;   God look down, with   glo - ry crown Our

conq-'ring band,   Vic - t'ry for   me,   Thro'   the Blood of

Christ, my Saviour, Vic - t'ry for   me,   thro' the prec-ious Blood.

(15)

8.

Holy Spirit, Seal Me, I Pray.

Words and Music by COMMANDANT H. H. BOOTH.

p Andantino.

1. Je - sus, my heart is pant-ing to ob - tain The
2. Seal Thou my heart, and al - ways let it cling To

full - ness of Thy Spir - it now; Oh,
ob - jects on - ly that are dear to Thee; Seal

cleanse my heart from ev - - 'ry stain, And
Thou my voice, and let it sing Of

leave Thy mark up - on my brow!
Thy un - chang - ing love for me.

Holy Spirit, Seal Me, I Pray.

CHORUS. *Allegretto con espress.*

Ho - ly Spir - it, seal me just now, At the cross help-less I

bow, I bow; On - ly like Je - sus, I long to be,

Ho - ly Spir - it, seal me, I pray! On - ly like Je - sus I

long to be, Ho - ly Spir - it, seal me, I pray!

3 Seal Thou my talents for Thy use
    alone,
  And let me spend my little all to
    bring
  The utmost credit to Thy throne,
  The utmost glory to my King.

4 Oh, seal me, Saviour, all I have and am,
  All offering freely laid before Thy
    feet;
  A follower of the bleeding Lamb,
  In thought and word for heaven
    made meet!

9.

Let Me Love Thee.

Words and Music by COMMANDANT H. H. BOOTH.

Andante con espress.

1 Let me love Thee, Thou art claim-ing Ev - 'ry
2. Let me love Thee— come re - veal - ing All Thy
3. Let me love Thee; love is might - y, Sway - ing

feel ing of my soul; Let that love in
love has done for me; Help my heart, so
realms of deed and thought; By it I shall

pow'r pre - vail - ing, Ren - der Thee my life, my
un - be - liev - ing, By the sight of Cal - va -
walk up - right - ly, I shall serve Thee as I

all, For life's bur - dens they are eas - y,
ry; Let me see Thy love de - spis - ing
ought. Love will soft - en ev - 'ry sor - row,

Let Me Love Thee.

And life's sor-rows loose their sting, If they're car - ried -
All the shame my sins had brought, By Thy tor - ments
Love will light-en ev - 'ry care, Love un - ques - tion-

Lord, to please Thee, If their pain Thy smile should win.
re - a - liz - ing, What a price my par - don bought.
ing will fol - low, Love will tri - umph, love will dare.

CHORUS.

Let me love Thee, Sav - iour, Take my heart for - ev - er;

Noth - ing but Thy fa - vor, My soul can sat - is - fy.

The Wounds of Christ.

Words and Music by COMMISSIONER EVA BOOTH.

p Andante con espress.   _cres._

1. { Dark shad-ows were fall-ing, My spir-it ap-pall-ing. For
   { And when I was weep-ing, The past o'er me creep-ing, I
2. { It soothes all life's sor-rows, It smoothes all its fur-rows, It
   { It turns night to morn-ing, So tru-ly a-dorn-ing. The

_mf_ 1   _mf_ 2

hid in my heart sin's deep crimson stains lay ; heard of the Blood which can
binds up the wounds which transgression has made ; spir-it with joy when all

CHORUS. _p Moderato._

wash sin a-way. }
oth-er lights fade. } The wounds of Christ are o-pen, Sinner, they were

made for thee ; The wounds of Christ are o-pen, There for ref-uge flee.

3 The current's first waking
    Was when Christ was taking
A world's shame and sorrow through
      death and the grave ;
    And angels were scheming
    To make out the meaning   [save.
To the hearts of all nations His power to

4 Come, cast in your sorrow,
    Wait not till to-morrow,
Life's evening is closing, the death-bell
      will toll ;
    His Blood for thee streaming,
    His Grace so redeeming,
His love intervening will pardon thy soul.

There Is A Better World.

Music by COMMANDER BOOTH TUCKER.

Moderato.

1. There is a bet-ter world, they say, O, so bright! O, so bright! O, so bright!

Where sin and woe are done a - way, O, so bright! O, so bright! O so bright!

And mu - sic fills the balm-y air, And an-gels with bright wings are there,

D.S.

And harps of gold and mansions fair, O, so bright! O, so bright! O, so bright!

2 And wicked things and beasts of prey,
    Come not there !
And ruthless death, and fierce decay,
    Come not there !
There all are holy, all are good.
But hearts unwashed in Jesus' blood,
And guilty sinners unrenewed,
    Come not there !

3 And though we're sinners every one,
    Jesus died !
And though our crown of peace is gone,
    Jesus died !
We may be cleansed from every stain,
We may be crowned with bliss again,
And in that land of glory reign,
    Jesus died !

12.

Promoted to Glory.

A Funeral Song.

By COMMANDANT H. H. BOOTH.

Andante sostenuto.

1. Yes! to the grave, But the crown as well, A comrade gone,
2. Take up the sword, It is left for you; Fill up the place,
3. Fire a sa-lute For a war-rior home; Lift up the flag

But in heav'n to dwell; Sor - row's night is end - ed,
It is of - fered too. Time is quick - ly fly - ing,
For a bat - tle won. Sa - tan's host re - treat - ed,

dim.

Je - sus' cause de-fend - ed, Gone the heav'nly choir to swell.
God for war-riors cry - ing, Will you not your du - ty do?
Death and hell de - feat - ed, Gone to hear the great "Well done!"

CHORUS. *mp cres.*

Vic - t'ry, vic - t'ry! Thro' the Blood of the Lamb that was slain!

Promoted to Glory.

mp cres.   *mf*

Vic - t'ry,   vic - tr'y! We shall meet in the morning to reign!

Chorus.

Words by F. W. FRY.

mp cres.

To Thy Cross I come, Lord! There for me is room, Lord,
Par - don ev - 'ry sin, Lord! Place Thy pow'r with-in, Lord,

mp cres.

mf

1.   **2.**

For un - wor-thy me,   e - ven me.   me.
Then I'll from this hour fol - low Thee.   Thee.

mf

13.

Going Down!

Words by CONSUL MRS. BOOTH TUCKER. Words & Music by COMMANDER BOOTH TUCKER.

mf Allegro moderato

1. Go - ing down with glad-ness at the Mas - ter's call, Go-ing
2. Go - ing down that I may weep with those who weep! Go-ing
3. Go - ing down to share the wid - ow's lone - ly lot! Go-ing
4. Go - ing down to make the slummer's dwell-ing neat! Go-ing

down to seek and save the worst of all, Go-ing down to bid the sinn-ing
down to depths of mis'ry still more deep! Go-ing down to hearts where long has
down that I may rock the outcast's cot! Go-ing down to clasp the or-phan
down to clothe the children's naked feet! Go-ing down where eyes of mer - cy

sin no more, Go - ing down to point their eyes to Canaan's shore.
reign'd des-pair! Go - ing down and, till I con-quer, stay-ing there.
to my breast! Toil-ing hard that I may bring the toil - ers rest!
sel - dom see! Go - ing down to make the poor a cup of tea.

CHORUS. *f*   *mf*

Blessed Je - sus! Je - sus! All the way with Jesus I will go;

I will go;

(24)

Going Down!

Blessed Je - sus! Je - sus! Nev - er to His voice will I say No!

5 Going down, though sorrow's tears our own eyes stain!
  Going down to watch by beds of deeper pain!
  Going down, though suff'ring may our own hearts weight!
  Going down when early! 'Going down when late!

6 Going down that I may send the lost ones up!
  Going down that bye and bye with Christ they'll sup!
  Going down while life shall last, still deeper down!
  Finding jewels precious for my Master's crown.

Let it Swing.

CHORUS.

This is where you'll find us, This is where we are, In the great S. A.

That led us when a - stray, In - to the nar - row way, And

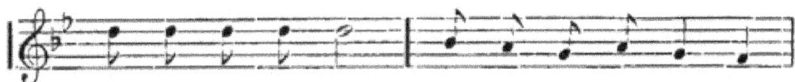

taught us how to pray, This is where you'll find us,

This is where we are, Gai - ly sing-ing on we mean to stay.

14.

Hasten Home Quickly.

Words by CONSUL MRS. BOOTH-TUCKER.   Music by COMMANDER BOOTH-TUCKER.

Andante. p

1. { Drea-ry, so drea-ry, Footsore and wea-ry, Wand'ring a-lone, a
   { Out on the mountain, Far from the foun-tain,

2. { On Thine ear fall-ing, Je-sus' voice call-ing, Bids thee return! Oh
   { With true con-tri-tion, Kneel in sub-mis-sion,

2. cres.   dim.

sin stricken soul.   Night's shadows falling. Death's bell soon will toll.
do not de-lay   Ask him to wash all the dark past a-way!

CHORUS. mf

Has-ten home quickly, Jesus will meet thee, With outstretch'd arms He's

waiting for thee.   All thy { transgressions } for-giv-en shall be.
                              { back-slid-ings }

3 Chances are flying !
  Life's days are dying !
Soon you will stand alone at God's Throne !
  All your professions,
  All your posessions
Will not avail you unless Blood atone.

4 If still rejected.
  Pardon neglected,
From you the Spirit will take His last flight !
  Hope then comes never !
  Shut out forever !
Lost in the gloom of eternity's night !

(26)

15.
Cleansing for Me.

Words by COMMANDANT H. H. BOOTH.

1. Lord, thro' the blood of the Lamb that was slain, Cleansing for me,
   From all the guilt of my sins now I claim. Cleansing for me.
2. From all the sins o-ver which I wept, Cleansing for me,
   Far, far a-way, by the blood current swept, Cleansing for me.

Cleansing for me; Sin-ful and black tho' the past may have been,
Cleansing for me. Je-sus, Thy promise I dare to be-lieve,

Ma-ny the crushing de-feats I have seen, Yet on Thy promise, O
And as I come Thou dost now re-ceive, And o-ver sin I may

Lord, now I lean, Cleans-ing for me, Cleans-ing for me.
nev-er more grieve, Cleans-ing for me, Cleans-ing for me.

3 From all the doubts that have filled me with gloom,
From all the fears that would point to my doom,
Jesus, although I may not understand,
In childlike faith now I put forth my hand,
And through Thy word and Thy grace I shall stand,
Cleansed by Thee.

4 From all the care of what men think or say,
From ever fearing to speak, sing, or pray,
Lord, in Thy love and Thy power make me strong,
That all may know that to Thee I belong;
When I am tempted let this be my song—
Cleansing for me.

(27)

16. A Wonderful Saviour is Jesus.

Words and Music by R. Slater.

1. I have glo-ri-ous ti-dings of Je-sus to tell, How
2. I have found that from fear He can free-dom be-stow, And
3. All the wealth of the bless-ing in Je-sus I hold, No
4. I am glad that the bless-ings the Lord gives to me, To

He un-to me has done all things well; And I love Him for stooping, in
o'er dark sorrow joy's radiance can throw; As a friend He can cheer one in
words ev-er spoken could ere un-fold; Like the waves of an o-cean up-
all who will ask Him are just as free; In His pit-y un-measured He

sin when I fell, Where His strong arm of mer-cy did reach me.
grief this I know, He in-deed is a won-der-ful Sav-iour.
on me are roll'd, Of His love all the rich-es un-bound-ed.
gra-cious will be Un-to all who will seek His Sal-va-tion.

CHORUS

A won-der-ful Saviour is Je-sus, Cleansing the soul, Making it whole;

A won-der-ful Saviour is Je-sus, I've prov'd He is mighty to save

(28)

17.

My Sins are Under the Blood.

Words and Music by F. W. Fry.

1. God's an-ger now is turned a-way, My sins are un-der the Blood.
2. My doubts are gone, the past forgiven, My sins are un-der the Blood.
3. How sweet the Lord's a-lone to be; My sins are un-der the Blood.

My darkness He has chang'd to day, My sins are un-der the Blood.
My title's clear, I'm bound for heav'n, My sins are un-der the Blood.
What joy to know He cleanses me, My sins are un-der the Blood.

CHORUS.

My sins. ..... my sins,.... my sins are un-der the Blood.

My sins, my sins are under the Blood, My guilt is gone, and my soul is free;

My peace, . my peace, . my peace is made with God.

My peace, my peace is made with God, For the Lord has par-doned me.

4 When sorrow's waves around me roll. My sins, etc.
In perfect peace He keeps my soul. My sins, etc.

5 In every step His hand doth lead, My sins, etc.
And He supplies my every need. My sins, etc.

6 What though the way I cannot see. My sins, etc.
Still this I know, He leadeth me. My sins, etc.

7 He'll keep me faithful to the end. My sins, etc.
And when in death He'll be my friend. My sins, etc.

God is Near Thee.

Words and Music by R. SLATER.

1. A - far from heav'n thy feet have wan - dered, A - far from
2. Thy feet have found sin's way is thorn - y, Thy heart has
3. The brok en heart the Lord will fa - vor, The con - trite
4. Tell out thy need, and He'll be - friend thee, Pour out thy

God thy soul has strayed: His gifts in sin thy hand has
found its pleas - ures vain: Thou hast grown wea - ry, and a -
spir - it He will bless: He came to be the lost one's
heart's deep grief to Him: His boundless love, un - meas - ured

squan - dered, Yet still in love He calls thee home.
bout thee, The gloom has spread of dark des - pair.
Sav - iour, He came to be the sin - ner's Friend.
mer - cy, His free for - giv - ness are for thee.

CHORUS. mf

God is near thee, tell thy sto - ry, He will hear thy tale of sor - row.

God is near thee, and in mer - cy, He will welcome thy re - turn.

From Every Stain Made Clean.

Andante. American Melody.

1. From ev-'ry stain made clean, From ev-'ry sin set free; Oh,
2. From Thee I would not hide My sin, be-cause of fear What
3. While in Thy light I stand, My heart I seem to see Has

bless-ed Lord, this is the gift, That Thou hast promised me.
men may think; I hate my pride, And as I am ap-pear.
failed to take from Thy own hand The gifts it of-fers me.

And press-ing thro' the past, Of fail-ure, falt, and fear, Be-
Just as I am, O Lord, Not what I'm thought to be; Just
O Lord, Thy plenteous grace, Thy wis-dom and Thy pow'r, I

Repeat for Chorus.

fore Thy cross my soul I cast, And dare to leave it there.
as I am, a strug-gling soul For life and lib-er-ty.
here pro-claim be-fore Thy face, Can keep me ev-'ry hour

4 Upon the altar here
  I lay my treasure down;
I only want to have Thee near,
  King of my heart to crown.
The fire doth surely burn
  My every selfish claim;
And while from them to Thee I turn,
  I trust in Thy great name.

5 A heart by Blood made clean,
  In every wish and thought;
A heart that by God's power has been
  Into subjection brought.
To walk, to weep, to sing,
  Within the light of Heaven:
This is the blessing, Saviour, King,
  That Thou to me hast given.

20. Over Me.

Words and Music by COMMISSIONER EVA BOOTH.

Moderato.

1. Bless-ed Lord, my past I bring, On Calvary's mer-cy ven-tur-
2. By the vir - tue of Thy grace, Thou canst my ma-ny sins ef-

- ing; My heart is torn, and my spir - it worn, With the
- face; Oh, hear my pray'r—save me from des - pair: In Thy

CHORUS.

strife and sor - row of sin. O - ver me, o - ver me, it is
wounds for me there's a place.

flow - ing, Down beneath its waves I am go - ing; O - ver

Over Me.

me, o-ver me it is flow-ing, Wash-ing white as snow.

3 All my idols now I cast
   Before Thy cross, and know Thou hast
   My past forgiven: By the claims of Heaven
   I, through Christ, have victory at last.

4 Now the Blood has set me free;
   Thy grace, dear Lord's enough for me,
   In all the strife of the battle life,
   Conqueror over sin I shall be.

Keep Me Unspotted from Sin.

CHORUS. *Allegro.* .　　　　　　　　Words and Music by BLIND MARK.

Keep me un-spot-ted from sin, dear Sav-iour, Keep me un-

spot-ted from sin, my Lord; I'll live for Thy glo-ry, And

tell out the sto-ry Of how Thou hast suf-fer'd and died.

B　　　　　　　　　(55)

21.

Oh, 'Twas Love.

Persian Melody.

Words by F. W. FRY.

1. Full of pit - y, love, and grace, Je - sus left His dwell-ing place,
2. He for me a curse was made, All my sins on Him were laid,

CHO.—*Oh 'twas love, 'twas wondrous love: Oh, 'twas love, 'twas wondrous love,*

And came on earth to dwell, And came on earth to dwell;
That I might pardoned be. That I might pardoned be;

The love of God to me, The love of God to me;

To save a lost and guilt - y world, From go - ing down to hell.
And from the guilt and pun - ish - ment, And power of sin be free.

It brought my Sav-iour from a - bove, To die on Cal - va - ry.

Repeat for Chorus.

To save a lost and guilt - y world, From go - ing down to hell.
And from the guilt and pun - ish - ment, And power of sin be free.

It brought my Sav-iour from a - bove, To die on Cal - va - ry.

3 He can Satan's works destroy,
Fill my soul with peace and joy,
Baptize me with His love,
And make me pure and holy here,
As angels are above.

4 Lord, I yield myself to Thee,
Let Thy will be done in me,
Oh, make me all Thine own,
And let my life henceforth proclaim
That I am Thine alone,

22.

I Love Him far Better.

Irish Melody.

Words by STAFF CAPTAIN ALBRI

1. There's a place that remembrance still brings back to me, 'Tis where I found
2. And oft when I'm tempted to turn from the track, I think of my
3. It pays to serve Je-sus, I speak from my heart, He'll ev - er be

par-don, 'tis heav-en to me; There Je-sus spoke peace to my
Sav-iour, my mind wan-ders back To the time when He suffered on
with us, if we do our part; There's nought in this world that can

FINE.

poor wea-ry soul, He forgave all my sin, and He made my heart whole.
Cal-va-ry's tree, And I hear a voice say-ing "I suffered for thee."
pleas-ure af-ford, But there's peace and contentment in serving the Lord.

D.S.—ev-er the cost, I'll be a true soldier,—I'll die at my post.

CHORUS.

I love Him f. bet-ter than in days yore, I'll serve Him more

D.S.

tru-ly than ev-er be-fore; I'll do as He bids me what-

23.

Power Divine!

Words and Music by COMMANDER BOOTH TUCKER.

mf Allegretto.

1. { Pow-er, dear Saviour, new pow-er I crave, Pow-er to suf-fer, to
{ Hearken, O Lord, to my Spir-it-taught-pray'r,

toil and to save; Grant me more pow-er to do and to dare.

f CHORUS.

Pow'r, pow'r, power divine! Pow'r, pow'r, Lord, be it mine! Power, Thy promise,

Pow-er, my plea, Lord, let Thy pow-er de-scend up-on me!

2 What though my trespasses pardoned have been,
   What though my heart by Thy Blood is made clean!
   Ne'er can my spirit's thirst satisfied be
   Till Thy blest power descends upon me.

3 Then, though earth's storm-waves may rage all around,
   Power shall keep me in heart-peace profound;
   Floods of temptation may over me roll,
   Thou shalt preserve me triumphant in soul.

Nothing but Thy Blood can Save Me.

Words and Music by MAJOR SLATER.

mf Andante con espress.

1. Je - sus, see me   at   Thy feet, Nothing but Thy blood can save   me:
2. See my heart, Lord, torn with grief, Nothing but Thy blood can save   me;
3. Dark in-deed the past has been, Nothing but Thy blood can save   me;
4. As I   am, oh, hear me pray! Nothing but Thy blood can save   me;

p

Thou a - lone my need canst meet, Nothing but Thy blood can save   me.
Me un-pard-oned do   not leave, Nothing but Thy blood can save   me.
Yet in mer - cy take me in,   Nothing but Thy blood can save   me.
I   can come no oth - er way, Nothing but Thy blood can save   me.

f CHORUS.

No!   no!   noth-ing do I bring, But by faith I'm cling - ing

mf

To Thy Cross, O Lamb of God; Nothing but Thy blood can save   me.

Ever Thine.

Words and Music by MAJOR R. SLATER.

1. Here before Thee, Lord, I'm bending, Ev'ry barrier broken by Thy love.
2. Be like Thine my words and actions; Be like Thine my motives and my aim;
3. By Thy foot-steps, dear Re-deemer I will trace my pathway here below;
4. If e'er grief my heart op-press-es, Pain and weariness bring me my cross,

And my heart that love con-strain-ing—Love re-turned to Thee would prove
So that all may see, with Je - sus I have been, and learn'd of Him
Deep in val-lay, high on moun-tains, An - y - where with Thee I'll go.
May I, Saviour, Thee re-mem - ber, Who didst suf - fer ev - 'ry loss

Chorus.

Ev - er Thine, Thine a - lone, Henceforth, Sav-iour, I will be;

This my hope, my life's am - bit - ion, Day by day to grow like Thee

26.

I'm Believing and Receiving.

Words and Music by COMMANDANT H. H. BOOTH

1. Sins of years are washed a-way, Blackest stains become as snow;
2. Doubts and fears are borne a-long, On the cur-rent's ceaseless flow;
3. Ease and wealth become as dross, Worthless, earth's delight and show;

Dark-est night is changed to day, When you to the riv-er go.
Sor-row chang-es in-to song, When you to the riv-er go.
All your boast is in the Cross, When you to the riv-er go.

CHORUS.

I'm be-liev-ing and re-ceiv-ing, While I to the riv-er go;

And my heart its waves are cleansing, Whiter than the driv-en snow.

4 Selfishness is lost in love,
Love for Him whose love you know;
All your treasure is above.
When you to the river go.

5 Fighting is a great delight,
Never will you fear the foe;
Armed by King Jehovah's might,
When you to the river go.

(39)

27. # Oh, Yes, There's Salvation for You.

1. O'er Co-lum-bia, from o-cean to o-cean, The Sal-va-tion Army you'll
2. We see how that sin's des-o-la-tion, Now threatens our land to de-
3. The out-cast, the drunkard bring hith-er, And all steeped in sin to the

see, Filled with love and a Sav-iour's de-vo-tion, Ev-'ry
form; On Je-sus, our rock and foun-da-tion, There's
brim; May zeal for our Mas-ter ne'er with-er, Nor de-

where slaves of sin set-ting free. Our meet-ings make man-y as-
safe-ty a-lone from the storm. With the Blood and Fire flags waving
sire for His glo-ry grow dim. May we from the Ar-my ne'er

sem-ble, Je-sus on-ly we lift up to view, And we'll
o'er us, Though on-ly a tried, faith-ful few, In the
sev-er, But ev-er to Je-sus prove true; Let

Oh, Yes, There's Salvation for You.

shout 'till we make Sat-an tremble, "Sinner, there is Sal-va-tion for you."
might of our Captain we'll conquer, Tell-ing all there's Salvation for you.
this be our war cry for ev-er. Sinner, there is Sal-va-tion for you.

Chorus.

Oh, yes, there's Salvation for you, Oh, yes, there's Salvation for you, For

you on the Cross Je-sus suf-fered, Sinner, there is Sal-va-tion for you.

Chorus.

p

Je-sus came with peace to me, His strong arm was stretched to me,

Then my bur-den took from me My Sa - viour.

28.

Bearing the Cross.

Words by MAJOR PEBBLES.

1. Je - sus, do hear me; may I speak to Thee?
2. Down in the gar - den, pray-ing there a - lone,
3. What of the cross, the nails, the spear, the crown;

Please, will you tell me how it could be?
An - gels were near Thee, why did you moan?
Why did the blood from your side flow down?

Why come from heav - en; why leave your Throne,
Big drops of blood, and grief in your tone,
Your hands were raised to bless, ev - 'ry time;

Weak, worn and hun - gry; no friend, no home?
God was not an - gry, why did you groan?
Who had con-demned you, what was your crime?

Bearing the Cross.

I saw the world in sin - ful - ness lie,
Great was the sin and guilt of the world,
I paid the price that sin - ners should pay,

Cursed by the law and con - demned to die;
Aw - ful the bur - den on Me was rolled;
I bore the stripes for sin - ners that day,

No eye to pit - y, no arm to save;
Could I so love them, their sins to bear,
I was heart-brok - en— bore all their blame,

I came to con - quer death and the grave.
Love was tri - umph - ant, love con - quered there.
They took the glo - ry, I took the shame.

Bearing the Cross.

CHORUS.

Bear - ing the cross of Je - sus, seek - ing to save the

lost; Stoop - ing to save the low - ly,

will - ing to pay the cost; Bear the re - proach of

Je - sus, faith - ful through sin's dark night, Je - sus will

crown you with glo - ry, af - ter the fight.

29.

The Rose of Sharon.

Words and Music by Mrs. HERBERT BOOTH.

1. I have found the Rose of Sharon, Af-ter seek-ing hour and day:
2. 'Tis the rar-est of all flow-ers, In the dark-ness shin-ing bright,
3. Have you found the Rose of Sharon? If not, seek it then, to-day;
4. Je-sus is the Rose of Sha-ron, A-bove all He is precious to me:

Ver-y wea-ry and lone did I wan-der, Till the flower was found on my way.
When in trouble, one look at it cheers me, When in anguish, one touch puts all right.
It is worth more than earth's boasted treasures, And its perfume makes easy life's way.
He's the rarest, the purest, the dearest, Oh, His face at the Cross you may see.

CHORUS.

I'm clinging like i-vy to Je-sus, From Him I nev-er will part;

No, nev-er! no, never from Him will I part;
No, nev-er! no, never from Him will I part.

(45)

Soldier, Rouse Thee.

1. { Sol - dier, rouse thee! war is rag - ing, God and fiends are
   { Dare ye still lie fond - ly dream ing, Wrapt in ease and

bat - tle wag - ing, Ev - 'ry ran - somed pow'r en - gag - ing.
world - ly schem - ing, While the mul - ti - tudes are streaming

CHORUS.

Break the temp - ter's spell. }
Down - ward in - to hell? }

Through the world re -

sound - ing, Let the Gos - ple sound - ing.

Soldier, Rouse Thee.

Sum-mon all at Je-sus' call, His glo-rious cross sur-round-ing: Sons of God, earth's tri-fles leav-ing, Be not faith-less, but be-lieve-ing, To your conquering Cap-tain cleav-ing, For-ward to the fight!

2 Lord, we come, and from Thee never
Self, nor earth our hearts shall sever;
Thine entirely, Thine forever,
    We will fight and die.
To a world of sinners dying,
Heaven, and hell, and God defying,
Every-where we'll still be crying—
    "Will ye perish—why?"

3 Hark! I hear the warriors shouting,
Now the hosts of hell we're routing;
Courage, onward, never doubting,
    We shall win the day.
See the foe before us falling,
Sinners on the Saviour calling,
Throwing off the bondage galling—
    Join our glad array.

31.

A Mother's Prayer.

1. "God bless my boy," prayed a fond moth - er,   Kneel-ing be - side
   But to that home there came a temp - ter,   From mother's heart

his trun-dle bed;   And an - gel guards their watch were keeping,
took him a - way;   Left her in   tears

E're that blest soul   her a - men had said;   mourn - ing his

dan - ger, Left her a - lone by the trun - dle to pray.

By per. Chas. K. Harris, Milwaukee, Wis.

A Mother's Prayer.

CHORUS.

There'll be   a   time   some   day,   When it's   too   late   to
No   one   to   in - ter - cede,   For your poor soul   to

pray;   There'll be   no   moth - er   be - side   you   kind
plead,   Then you'll re - mem - ber   I   told

words   to   say,   you,   There'll come   a   time.

2 "Bless you my boy," prayed a fond mother,
   Weeping he knelt by her death bed:
   "Meet me in heaven, promise me faithful."
   "I'll meet you there, mother," he said:
   But ere the flowers on her grave withered
   He had forgot his pledge that day;
   "Some time," said he, "I'll turn to Jesus."
   So he went on in the old, old way.

3 "Lord save this soul," thus prayed a Captain;
   Kneeling beside a dying man;
   "Pardon the past, Lord in Thy mercy,
   Save him just now, save if You can."
   "It is too late now, I am dying,
   I am so cold, God is not near.
   Oh, mother dear, if I had heeded,
   Why did I leave you when you were here."

(49)

32.   Speak, Saviour, Speak!

(Secular Melody.)

p Andante.

1. Let me hear Thy voice now speaking,   Let me hear and I'll o - bey;
2. Let me hear and I   will fol-low, Tho' the path be strew'd with thorns;
3. Let the blood of Christ for ev - er   Flood and cleanse my heart within:

While be - fore Thy Cross I'm seeking,   Oh, chase my fears a - way.
It   is   joy   to share Thy sor-row,   Thou mak - est calm the storms.
That to grieve Thee I   may nev - er   More stain my soul with sin.

mf

Oh,   let   the light now fall-ing   Re - veal my ev - 'ry need;
Now my heart Thy tem-ple making,   In Thy fulness dwell with me;
Fare - well   to world-ly pleasure,   Fare - well   to self and pride;

Now   hear   me while I'm call-ing,   Oh! speak, and I   will heed.
Ev-'ry   e - vil way for - sak-ing,   Thine on - ly I   will be.
How   wondrous is   my treasure,   With Je - sus at   my side!

Speak, Saviour, Speak!

p Chorus.

Speak, Sav-iour, speak! O - bey Thee I will ev - er;

Now at Thy Cross I seek From all that's wrong to sev - er.

All I Need I in My Saviour Find.

Chorus.

All I need I in my Sav - iour, find, All I

need I in my Sav - iour find, He has wash'd me throughly,

rit.

I will love Him tru - ly, All my need is ful - ly met in Him.

Right Away.

Words by COMMISSIONER RAILTON.

Tune.—"Dixie."

1. Oh, ev-'ry land is fill'd with sin, But The Sal-va-tion Ar-my is
2. So north and south, and east and west, The cour-age of the dev-il's

bound to win, Right a-way, right a-way, right a-way, right a-way.
host we'll test. Right a-way, right a-way, right a-way, right a-way.

CHORUS.

We mean to fight for Je-sus! We will! we will! we will! we will!

In ev-'ry land we'll take our stand, And live and die for Je-sus.

We will! we will! we will! we will! We'll live and die for Je-sus!

3 We care for nothing but saving souls,
And by Gods help we'll have them by shoals.
4 We'll bring the women right out to the front, [shunt.
And make the cowards and the doubters

5 We'll march with song and band and flag,
And godless crowds to the Cross we'll drag.
6 Our Jesus saves from sin and fear,
And He can sanctify men down here.

34.

The Soul's Independence Day.

Words and Music by COMMANDER BOOTH TUCKER.

1. { Hell's legions have gathered, Sin's cannon have boomed, O'er earth's brightest regions
From Cal-va-ry's mountain Sounds forth the a-larm!

Death's tempest hath loomed! Haste, haste to the battle! Arm, miuute men, arm!

CHORUS.

Speed, speed to the con - flict In bat - tle ar - ray!

Sol - diers of Sal - va - tion, Go forth to the fray!

2 Scorn earth's false ambitions,
   Tread down its delights!
Go rescue world-millions!
   Restore them their rights!
Burn bridges behind you.
   Snap self's strongest chain!
Charge, charge on the foemen
   Till vict'ry you gain!

3 Hark! loudly is ringing
   Heaven's Liberty Bell!
Glad millions rejoicing,
   Joy's anthem-song swell!
Sin's fetters are shattered!
   Hell's captives are free!
Blood-bought independence!
   Christ-giv'n liberty!

Pardon Through the Blood.

Words by R. SLATER.

p *Allegro* con espress.

1. { Dark .. is the way,..... sin-ner, which ... thou hast tak
   { joice..... for the Sav - - iour has not...... thee for - sak -

cres.

en, Thy ..... heart is wea - ry, ' grief and woe it has
en, Still..... He is

known; But re - call - ing thee, to Him for pardon, O come.

f CHORUS.

There's par-don for all who turn to our God, There's par-don for

Pardon Through the Blood.

cres.

all thro' the Blood......... That Je - sus shed free - ly,

When in His mer - cy, He for the sin - ner was slain......

2 Turn from thy sin and from God ask for favor,
   Tread not the way that leadeth on to despair;
Oh, be glad that in Jesus for thee there's a Saviour,
   Come to Him, guilty one, to Him for pardon draw near.

3 Days brighter far, by God's grace are before thee,
   Strength He will give, and keep thy soul from each stain;
Then for pardon of sin venture now on His mercy,
   To Him thy burden bring, from Him thy pardon, oh, claim.

Chorus.

Words and Music by CAPT. J. C. BATEMAN.

Cal-va-ry's stream is flow-ing, Cal-va-ry's stream is flowing.

Flowing so free For you and me, Cal-va-ry's stream is flow-ing.

Satisfied.

Words and Music by CAPT. THERON M. PERSONS.

1. I know the path . . . . . . of pleas-ure well, ...
   I care not what . . . . the peo-ple say, ...

I know the end, ... it leads to hell; . . . .
For in the war . . . . I am to-day; . . . .

I know the power . . . . that breaks the spell, ...
I mean to fight . . . . in the Army way, ...

Of Sa - - - - tan and of sin.
Till we . . . . the vic - tory win.

Satisfied.

Chorus.

Oh, hal - le - lu - jah! hal - le - lu - jah! I am glad to tell;

Oh, hal - le - lu - jah! hal - le - lu - jah! With my soul 'tis well!

2 A Christless life is all in vain,
Just so a life of worldly gain;
Then seek the Saviour, and obtain
  That power to make you whole.
Christ gives it to the rich and poor,
He spreads His love from door to door,
And when the toils of life are o'er,
  You'll find He saves the soul.

3 I'm happy as I journey on,
Through life I'll sing the victor's song,
And then I know it won't be long,
  Before I'll see my Lord.
And then I feel I shall rejoice,
That e'er I listened to His voice,
And did not make a worldly choice,
  But rather served my God.

All My Heart Belongs to Jesus.

Words and Music by MAJOR R. SLATER.

Chorus. *mf*

All my heart belongs to Je - sus, He died for me on Cal - va - ry;

All my heart belongs to Je - sus, I love Him, yes, more and more.

(57)

37.

It's True There's a Beautiful City.

1. It's true there's a beauti-ful cit-y, That it's streets are pav'd with gold:

No earth-ly tongue can describe it, Its glo-ries can nev-er be told --

CHORUS.

But I know!.... I know!....

I know! I know! I know I shall be

I know! I know!

there! I know! I know! I know I shall be there!

2 Those loved ones dwell in that city,
  Whom you placed beneath the sod,
When your heart felt nigh to breaking,
  And you promised you'd serve your God—
    Will you? will you?
      Say, **will you** meet them there?

3 There **none but** the pure and holy
  Can ever enter in ;
You have **no** hope of it's Glory,
  If still you're the servant of sin—
    Bless God ! Bless God!
      Bless God, you may be there!

4 Yes, you can go there, my brother,
  For Jesus has died on the tree ;
And that same precious Blood is now flowing
  That washed a poor sinner like me—
    Will you? will you?
      Will you now wash and **be clean?**

5 All who enter that glorious city,
  Have made their garments white ;
Have trod in the Saviour's footsteps,
  They've battled for God and the right—
    I long ! I long!
      I long to meet you there!

38.

My Lord, what a Mourning.

mp Moderato.

1. You'll see the Great White Throne, And stand before it all a - lone:
2. Be - fore the Judg-ment Seat, Your sentence will the King re - peat!
3. You'll see the King come forth, To judge the na - tions in His wrath!
4. You'll hear Him say, "Well done!" To all who have the bat - tle won;

Wait-ing for the King to call, When the stars be - gin to fall!
Ter - ror will you then en - thral, When the stars be - gin to fall!
Sin - ners to the rocks will call When the stars be - gin to fall!
Oh, that He may claim us all, When the stars be - gin to fall!

CHORUS. *mf*

My Lord! what a mourning! My Lord! what a
My Lord! what a mourning! My Lord!

mourning! My Lord! *cres.* *f*

what a mourning! My Lord! what a mourning, When the stars begin to fall!

(59)

39. The March to the Golden Shore.

Words and Music by COMMANDANT H. H. BOOTH.

mf Allegro.

1. Come a - way while the riv - er of His grace is flow - ing, Wash in the current and be clean, While He waits, His compassion and His patience showing, Ask for for-giv-ness, on His prom - ise lean. Tho' of sin - ners you may be the chief - est, Tho' your life is burden'd with its shame, There is hope is re - pent-ing thou be - liev - - - est, Trust the pow'r of Christ's great name.

2. Come a - way, for the time is short and quick - ly fly - ing, Soon will your chance of peace be gone; Will you lin - ger, His patience and His love de-ny-ing, Lin - ger till grace is past and judgment come? Let the pow'r of Cal - va-ry's blest sto - ry, Let it now in - vite your soul a - way; Come and march in our hap - py ranks to glo - - - ry, To the realm of end - less day.

(60)

The March to the Golden Shore.

f Chorus.

Sin - ner, leave your shame and sin, In our ranks we'll take you in, For the

Marcato.

march to the gold - en shore; Je - sus saves us all the day, And He

leads us all the way, To the vic - to - ry for ev - er - more.

ff

Come, come, come, come! Mer - cy now is free - ly flow - ing,

Marcato.

f 1.

Sin - ner, come a - way! Come be-fore the dawning of the Judgment Day!

f 2.

(G1)

The Three Bidders for the Soul.

Words and Music by BANDSMAN COLLER, (Regent Hall.)

mp Moderato.

1. In bright an - gel - ic garb ap - pear- ing, With words so seemingly di-
2. The world with man-i - fold at - trac - tions, Is al - so bidding for thy

vine, In ac - cents sub - tle and en - dear - ing, The Tempter
soul; O give me now thy heart's af - fec - tions, I'll bring thee

1. "I of - fer thee............ earth's brightest
2. Is wealth and glo - - - ry thy am-

bids thee to his shrine. "I offer thee earth's brightest
to thy cherished goal. Is wealth and glo-ry thy am-

treas-ure, A sun-ny sky,............ a smil-ing sea,......... ...
bi - tion? Is it to fame............ thou dost as-pire,............

treas-ure, A sun - ny sky, a smil-ing sea, a smil-ing sea,
bi - tion? Is it to fame thou dost aspire, thou dost aspire?

The Three Bidders for the Soul.

A brimming cup.............. of sweetest pleas - ure, If thou wilt
If thou wilt close .... with my con - di - tion, I'll give thee

A brimming cup of sweetest pleas - ure, If thou wilt
If thou wilt close with my con - di - tion, I'll give thee

CHORUS.

fall   and worship me."   Choose ye to-day, 'tis the Spirit's pleading voice;
all   thy heart's de sire.

Choose ye to-day, make the Saviour now your choice; Je- sus a- lone can your

crav-ing heart rejoice. Choose ye to- day ere the Spir-it pass a- way.

3.
One Bidder more thy choice is waiting,
  He yearns, He claims thee as His own !
" Child of My heart, why hesitating ?
  For thee I left the Father's throne.
For thee I trod the path of anguish,
  For thee endured the crown of thorn,
Through death and darkness I did languish
  To bring to thee a brighter dawn."

4.
Thou bleeding Lamb, Thy love has broken
  This stony heart, my choice is made;
The deed is done, Thy Blood the token,
  My all is on Thine altar laid;
The Tempter's share, the World's alluring,
  Shall never draw me from Thy side,
Henceforth for Thee the worst enduring,
  I'll dwell beneath Thy riven side.

41.

Long o'er the Mountains.

p Andante con espress. (Verse as a SOLO *or* DUET*.)*

1. Long o'er the mountains My poor soul has gone a - stray,   In black - est
2. My soul heard Thy wooing Yet sped on its mad ca - reer;   Sa - tan de -

darkness, Dreaming 'twas day. Hast'ning fast to destruction, Dreaming
ceiv - ing, Said, "Hope is near." Pass-ing by all warn - ing, Yet my

still that all was well, Oh, so heed-less of danger, Go-ing-down to hell.
soul would heave a sigh; Thy clear voice still pleading— "Why wilt thou die?

p CHORUS.

But Je - sus, dear Je - sus, You were ev - er at my
Sin - ner, poor sin - ner, Wilt thou still my love de -

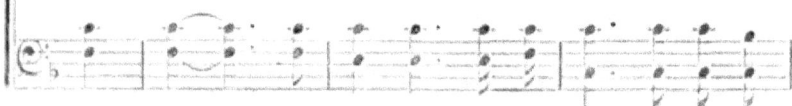

(64)

Long o'er the Mountains.

side,   En - treat - ing   and   plead-ing—   For   thee   I   died!"
fy?   Sin - ner,   poor   sin - ner....   Why   wilt   thou   die?"

3 Roused from my dreaming,
   My souls eyes were open wide—
Hell frowned before me,
   Remorse my guide;
My sad heart relenting,
   While my sins rose mountains high,
Satan still hissing—
   "Your time's gone by!"

Then Jesus, dear Jesus'
   On the tree uplifted high,
Whispered so sweetly—
   "You need not die!"

4 Then joy, like sunbeams
   Breaking through the clouded sky
Sweet light in the darkness,
   Bright hope drew nigh;
Sweet the voice now pleading,
   Coming from the rugged tree,
And with blood still streaming,
   Cried, "I die for thee!"

'Twas Jesus, my Jesus,
   Crying, "Sinner, look to Me!"
My heart was broken,
   My spirit free!

Chorus.

Words and Music by Major R. Slater.

Near- er, yes nearer my Sav-iour, Oh! draw me yet nearer   to   Thee.

Near- er, yes near-er my Sav- iour, And per-fect Thy likeness in   me.

C

42. Bless Our Army!

Tune—"Just Before the Battle."

1. O Thou God of ev-'ry na-tion,
   Fit us for full con-se-cra-tion,
2. Fill us with Thy Ho-ly Spir-it,
   Save the world through Je-sus' mer-it,

We now Let the
Make our
Sa-tan's

for Thy bless-ing call;
fire from Heav-en fall;
sol-diers white as snow;
king-dom o-verthrow.

Bless our Arm-y! Bless our Arm-y!
Bless our Arm-y! Bless our Arm-y!

With Thy pow'r bap-tise us all,
Send us where we ought to go,

Bless our Arm-y! Bless our
Bless our Arm-y! Bless our

Arm-y! With Thy pow'r bap-tise us all.
Arm-y! Send us where we ought to go.

3 Give the world more holy living,
   Fill it with abundant power;
Give the Army more thanksgiving,
   Greater victories every hour.
   Bless our Army!
Be our Rock, our Shield, our Tower

4 Bless our General, bless our leaders,
   Bless our officers as well;
Bless Headquarters, bless our soldiers,
   Bless the foes of sin and hell.
   Bless our Army!
We will of Thy goodness tell.

43. I Cannot Leave The Dear Old Flag.

Tune—"We'd Better Bide a Wee"

By COMMANDER BOOTH TUCKER.

1. { They bid me choose an eas-ier path, And seek a bright-er cross ; They
    bid me min-gle with Heav'ns gold A (Omit.) ....
2. { They say the fight-ing is too hard, That health will sure-ly fail, That
    dread-ful is a pau-per's lot My (Omit.) ....

lit- tle of earths dross! They bid me, but in vain, once more The worlds il-
face, they say, looks pale ! But oh, how can I quit my post, While mil-lions

lu - sions try! I can-not leave the dear old Flag, 'Twere better far to
sin-bound lie ? I can-not leave the dear old Flag, 'Twere better far to

die! I can - not leave the dear old Flag, 'Twere better far to die!
die! I can - not leave the dear old Flag, 'Twere better far to die !

3 They say I can a Christian be,
  And serve God quite as well.
And reach Heav'n just as surely by
  The music of church-bell !
But, oh, the drum and clarion call
  Of band make my pulse fly !
I cannot leave the dear old Flag,
  'Twere better far to die !

4 I answer, life is fleeting fast,
  I cannot, cannot wait !
For me my comrades beckoning stand
  Beyond the Pearly Gate !
I hear their Hallelujahs grand !
  I hear their battle-cry !
Oh, do not leave the dear old Flag,
  'Twere better far to die !

Have Faith in God.

Words and Music by MAY AGNEW

1. Do you ev - er feel down-heart - ed or dis - cour - aged?
2. Dark - est night will al - ways come be - fore the dawn - ing,

Do you ev - er think your work is all in vain?
Sil - ver lin - ings shine on God's side of the cloud;

Do the bur - dens thrust up - on you make you trem - ble,
All your jour - ney He has prom - ised to be with - you,

And you fear that you shall ne'er the vic - t'ry gain?
Naught has come to you but what His love al - lowed.

Have Faith in God.

Have faith in God, ... The sun will shine, ...
Have faith in God, The sun will shine,

Tho' dark the clouds .... May be to - day, ...
Tho' dark the clouds May be to - day,

His heart has planned .... Your path and mine; ....
His heart has planned Your path and mine;

Have faith in God, ... Have faith al - way. ....
Have faith in God, Have faith alway.

To Heal the Broken Heart He Came.

Words and Music by MAJOR R. SLATER.

mp Andante con express.

1. A bid-ing place from ev-'ry storm, A shel-ter that defends from harm,
2. O wounded heart, thy sorrow bring, For thou may'st gain relief from Him,
3. O trembling one, thy heav-y weight Of guilt just now to Je-sus take;
4. Thy bonds shall break, O captive one, For Christ to set thee free has come;

A light that cheers the path of gloom, Is Christ to all who to Him come.
Who gave His life so to re-deem Each grie-ving soul o'er-thrown by sin.
He shed His blood that He might make A cleansing fount-ain for thy sake.
He waits to give the precious boon—The freedom thou hast sought so long.

p Chorus. *dolce.*

To heal the brok - - en heart He came, ... To free the
He came to heal the broken heart,

cap - - - tive from his chain; . . The blood He spilt . . . .
From ev-'ry chain each soul to free; The blood He spilt,

cres *rit.* *f*

when He was slain, Brings guilt-y sin-ners home to God.
when He was slain,

(70)

46.

Liberty Bell!

Words and Music by Commander Booth Tucker.

1. Send thy re - frain O'er hill and plain, Lib-er - ty Bell! Lib-er- ty Bell!
2. Thro' endless time How sweet thy chime, Lib-er - ty Bell! Lib-er- ty Bell!
3. With gladness still, How thy notes thrill! Cal-va- ry Bell! Cal-va- ry Bell!

Let nations sing, Let the world ring With thy glad tidings o'er mountain and dell!
Bursting sin's chain, Cleansing each stain, Freeing each captive from sin's prison cell!
Down at the Cross, Earth seems as dross, While thy sweet echoes athwart my soul swell!

CHORUS.

1.&2. Lib-er-ty Bell! Lib-er-ty Bell! Peal out thy music o'er mountain and dell!
3. Cal-va- ry Bell! Cal-va-ry Bell! Peal out thy music e'er mountain and dell!

Lib-er-ty Bell! Lib-er-ty Bell! Hasten each sinner thy message to tell!
Cal-va-ry Bell! Cal-va-ry Bell! Hasten each sinner thy message to tell!

(71)

Rolled Away.

Words and Music by COMMANDANT H. H. BOOTH.

1. Out up-on the broad way speed-ing With the husks my poor soul feed-ing
2. Fast from hope and mer-cy sink-ing, I the bit-ter cup was drinking;
3. I had wandered long in sad ness, Blind-ed by my sin and mad-ness;

Je-sus came, and sought, and found me, And my bur-den, all my bur-den, All my
Till in love my Sav-iour met me, And my dark-ness, all my dark-ness, All my
Till by love my heart was bro-ken, And my sor-row, all my sor-row, All my

CHORUS.

Rolled a-way, rolled a-way,

bur-den rolled a-way
dark-ness turned to light.
sorrow changed to song.

Rolled a-way. rolled a-way, Oh, the

Rolled a-way, rolled a-

bur-den of my heart rolled a-way, rolled a-way, Rolled a-way,

way.

rolled a-way, Oh, the bur-den of my heart, Of my heart rolled a way.

(72)

Far Away Across the Sea.

mp Con espress.

1. Far a - way a - cross the sea, Where the fields are bright and fair,
2. Hark, I hear the Mas-ter say, "Up, ye reap - ers! Why so slow?
3. Just be - yond the roll-ing tide, The up - lift - ed hand I see;
4. Bear me o'er the rest - less sea, Let the winds the can-vass swell;

There's a call, a plain-tive plea, I must has - ten to be there.
In my vine - yard, far a - way, There's a work for you to do!"
Lo, the gates are opened wide, And the lost are call - ing me.
In - dia's shores I long to see; Dear-est land, fare-well! fare - well!

f CHORUS.

Let me go! I can-not stay, 'Tis the Mas - ter who doth call!

Let me go! I must o - bey! Lord, for Thee I give up all.

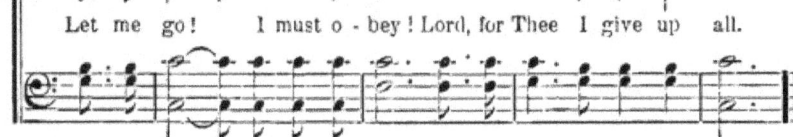

49.

Papa will You Meet Me?

Words and Music by STAFF CAPT. ADAMS.

p Andante.

1. The night was dark and storm-y, the wind was howl-ing wild, With
2. An a-ged mother full of care, lay breath-ing out her last, The
3. A dar-ling wife and moth-er, her race on earth had run, And

In a hum-ble cot-tage, there lay a dy-ing child, The waves of deaths dark-
glassy eye, and hurried pulse, told death was com-ing fast, Her hair was white, her
to the deep dark riv-er, a faith-ful wife had come, A-round the bed-side

riv-er, were ris-ing fast and sure, To bear the frail bark o-ver, to
hand was thin, her brow in fur-rows lay, As to yon home of glo-ry, her
gathered her chil-dren, one by one, And with his hand lock'd tight in hers, a

you E-ter-nal Shore, { Be-side the form there lingered, the parents good and
{ With aching hearts and tearful eyes, they gen-tly led her

soul was borne a-way, { But in her heart and in her mind, a heav-y sor-row
{ Her wandering boy so far a-way, had brought her sad dis-

weeping husband stands, { He has not been so kind to her, as when they first were
{ In-to a life of sin and drink, with gid-dy crowds had

Papa will You Meet Me?

true. :|| through, The gates of pain and sor - row, they wipe the sweat a -
press'd, :|| tress, She gen - tly breathes a whis-per. ere life its pa - ges
wed, :|| sped. But listen to her pleading tones, as she lies dy - ing

way, While soft - ly from the lips there came, a voice which thus did say, Oh,
end. And this is what the mes - sage was to God she oft did send.
there. These words fall heav - y on his heart, as she re - peats this pray'r, Oh,

CHORUS pp

Pa - pa will you meet me, where no sor-row ev - er comes, Ma - ma will you
Wil - lie will you meet me, where no sor-row ev - er comes, Wil - lie, will you
hus-band will you meet me, where no sor-row ev - er comes, Husband will you

join me in yon choir of an - gel tongues, Meet me in yon home of love, join me

in the throng a bove, (Pa-pa / Willie / Pa-pa) promise you'll meet me, Be - fore I say good-bye.

50.

At Thy Feet I Fall.

Words by THE MARECHALE.

mp Andante.

1. O Lamb of God! Thou won-der-ful sin-bear-er, Hard af - ter Thee my
2. I mourn, I mourn, the sin that drove Thee from me, And blackest darkness
3. Descend the heav'ns, Thou whom my soul adoreth! Oh, come just now, till
4. Come, Ho-ly Ghost, Thy mighty aid be-stow-ing, De-stroy the works of

soul doth fol-low on; As pants the hart for streams in desert drea-ry, So
brought in-to my soul; Now I renounce the cursed sin that hindered, And
my poor longing breast; For Thee! for Thee! I watch, as for the morning; A-
sin, the self, the pride; Burn, burn in me, my i-dols o-ver-throwing; Pre-

mf CHORUS.

pants my soul for Thee, O Thou life giv-ing One.
come once more to Thee, to be made full-ly whole.
part from Thee, I find nei-ther joy, peace, nor rest.
pare my heart for Him—for my Lord cru-ci-fied.
} At Thy feet I fall,

Yield Thee up my all, To suf-fer, live or die For my Lord cru-ci-fied.

51. Saviour, My All I Surrender.

Andante con espress.

Words and Music by R. SLATER.

1 Of-ten Thy voice I have heard Lord, Asking me ful-ly to yield all to
2 Wea-ry of half-hearted ser-vice, Low at Thy feet, Saviour, see now I
3. I will no long-er go seek-ing How I may find, Lord, an eas-i-er

Thee; Tho' I've re-sist-ed Thy plead-ing, Yet once a-gain Thou art
bow; Lift from my soul, Lord, its bur-den, Oh, let the cleans-ing tide
road Than that one which Thou hast tak-en, Joy-ful-ly do-ing the

mf CHORUS.

speak-ing to me. }
reach me just now. } Sav-iour, my all I sur-ren-der, Sin no
will of my God. } Sav-iour, my all I sur-ren-der, Let Thy

1 long-er from Thee shall my spirit divide; 2 Blood to my heart be applied:

4 Put, Lord, Thy spirit within me;
   Cause me on earth in Thy footsteps
      to tread;
   Oh, let me taste of that pleasure
      That fills the heart whence self-seek-
         ing has fled.

5 Glory to Thee, blessed Saviour!
   Thou hast in mercy accepted my
      heart:
   Strong in Thy grace I go forward,
      Glad that from sin Thou hast helped
         me to part.

With Sword and Shield.

Words and Music by COMMANDANT H. H. BOOTH.

mf Allegro.

1. We are march-ing o'er the re-gions Where the sla - ve - ry of sin
2. Have you heard the voice of weeping, Have you heard the wail of woe,
3. In the dark-est hour re-mem-ber Him who on the Cross has died;

Is en-forced by hell - ish le-gions, But we'll fight and we shall win.
Have you seen the fear - ful reap-ing, Of a soul that sinks be-low?
So that ev - 'ry cap-tive's fet-ter Might be brok - en, cast a - side!

f

Step by step we march a - long, Nev - er daunt-ed, fear - ing
Rouse, then, who by Christ are freed, Heed, oh heed the world's great
Grip your weap - ons, Sol - diers brave, For - ward, dy - ing souls to

none; True lib - er - ty from self and Sa - tan, Is our song.
need, To save the lost, like Him who saved you, For - ward speed!
save! Fight on, un - till in ev - 'ry land Your col - ors wave!

With Sword and Shield.

With sword and shield we take the field, We're not a-fraid to die, While the

standard of the Cross is waving o'er us; We raise on high our battle cry, And

all hell's pow'rs defy, Scatter'd by our ranks, the foe falls down before us.

March on! March on! Heed not the can-non's roar;

Marcato.

March on! March on! There's a crown when the battle's o'er.

One With My Lord.

Words and Music by COMMANDANT HERBERT BOOTH.

p Andante con moto.

1. One with my Lord! 'tis glo-rious to know The barriers are broken and gone:
2. One with my Lord! with His purpose and will—so one that I ne'er can com-plain;
3. One with my Lord! with His toil and His care, In seek-ing and sav-ing the lost,
4. One with my Lord! with His Cross and His shame, With the mocking, the spear and the thorn;

mf

Wher-ev- er He leadeth, there gladly I'll go; Yes, I and King Je-sus are ONE.
My bus'ness down here His words to ful- fil, My PURPOSE to hon-our His Name.
Re-memb'ring when looking on those in despair, How to save them His life-blood it cost,
Won by His love, I have taken His name —Should I leave Him because of earth's scorn?

CHORUS. *mp*

Je - sus with me is u - ni - ted, Doubtings and fears are all gone;

With Him now my soul is de-light - ed, I and King Je-sus are one.

5	6
One with my Lord! when time has gone by And eternity opens to view, On His grace and His strength I then will rely, And trust Him to carry me through.	One with my Lord! on the throne of His might I shall take my place by His side. And then in that land of rapture and right With HIM I'll for ever abide.

Let Them Come!

Words and Music by COMMANDER BOOTH-TUCKER.

mf Andantino.

1. "Let the lit - tle ones come un - to Me! ... Said the Sav-iour," and
2. "Let the lit - tle ones come un - to Me!.... There is room for them
3. Let them come in the morn of their life,.... While the bit - ters of
4. Let them all in My ser - vice u - nite, ... O'er their heads be My

hin-der them not.... For in heav-en My Fa - ther they see, And on
all in My Arm; In My bo-som a - lone can they be Safe-ly
sin are un - known, Unbestained by earth's sorrow and strife— Let Me
banner un - furled; For My kingdom on earth bid them fight,Urge them

D.S.—Where the face of My Fa - ther they see, And re-

FINE. *f* CHORUS.

earth too, not one is for - got."
guard-ed from dan - ger and harm."
seal their young hearts as My own. } "Let them come unto Me, My dis -
on- ward to save a lost world.
joice in His in - fin - ite love.

D.S.:S:

ci - ples to be. For of such is My king-dom a - bove, ...

(81)

55. # I have Read of Men of Faith.

Words by BLIND MARK.

1. I have read of men of faith, Who have bravely fought till death,
2. I will join at once the fight, Leaving on my Saviour's might,
3. Will you not en - list with me, And a gal - lant sol - dier be?

Who now the crown of life are wear-ing: Then the tho't comes back to
Who's strong and mighty to de - liv - er; From my post I will not
Vain 'tis to waste your time in slum-ber; Je - sus calls for men of

me, Can I not a sol-dier be, Like to those martyrs bold and daring?
shrink, Tho' I of death's cup should drink; Hell to defeat is my endeavor.
war, Who will fight and ne'er give o'er, Routing hell's hosts in fear and wonder.

CHORUS.

I'll gird on my ar-mour and rush to the field, De - termined to

I Have Read of Men of Faith.

conquer and nev - er to yield; So the en - e - my shall know, Whereso-

ev - er I may go, That I am fight-ing for Je - ho - vah.

Oh, the Crowning Day is Coming!

Words and Music by MAJOR R. SLATER.

CHORUS.

Oh, the crowning day is com-ing, Hal - le - lu - jah! Oh, the

crowning day is coming, Praise the Lord! For our Saviour King shall reign,

He shall have his own a - gain, Hal - le - lu - jah! Hal - le - lu - jah!

Who's That Knocking at the Door?

F. W. FRY.

1. You have oft heard the call to sur - ren - der, God's Spir - it with
2. His voice you have long dis- re - gard - ed, Un - heed - ed, He's
3. There's a time com-ing on when you'll want Him To bear you safe
4. When He comes as a Bridegroom at mid-night, No time to pre -

you oft has striv'n; Now a - gain to your heart He is speak - ing.
knocked at the door; Sin - ner, now o - pen wide to thy Sav - iour,
o-ver death's stream; Then be wise, and in time seek His fav - or,
pare you will find; Then you'll knock, but in vain for ad - mit - tance,

CHORUS.

And an - oth - er blest of - fer is giv'n.
Lest He leave thee, to knock never more.
And just now while He knocks let Him in.
He will leave you in darkness be - hind.

Who's that knocking at the

door, at the door? Who's that knocking at the door, at the door? 'Tis

Je - sus there, oh, sinner hear, Let Him in while He's waiting at the door.

57.   * The Warrior's Farewell!

Words and Music by COMMANDER BOOTH TUCKER.

1. Now the sword is chang'd for crown, Now the battle's din doth cease! Warrior lay thy weapon
pearly gates swing wide. Loud the Hal-le-lu-jahs ring! Angel hands the victor

down, En-ter in to Heaven's peace! Lo, the
guide, An-gel voi-ces wel-come sing.

CHORUS   mf

Quick step, Forward! March our grand batalions! Quick step, Forward! To the Promis'd Land!

Quick step, Forward! March our grand batalions! Thro' death's Riv - er,   hand in hand!

2 'Tis not death when heroes die,—
'Tis not death, but life begun,
No more darkness dims their sky,
Never sets their dazzling sun:
Tearless eyes and spotless grace,
Fadeless joys and boundless power,
Their's who see Him face to face,
Serve their Saviour hour by hour.

3 Soon for us will come the call,
Soon for us the chariot speed!
Soon on life the curtain fall,
Soon from earth our soul be freed;
Let each moment sacred be,—
Let me live as I would die!
Bring the lost, dear Lord, to Thee,
Til I meet Thee in the sky!

* NOTE — Jesus, Lover of My Soul, may be sung to the same tune.

58.

The Song of the Ages.

Words and Music by R. Slater.

mf Vivace.

1. The Sol-diers of the Cross on earth as well as those in heav'n, One
2. The throng that stand before the throne with victor's palms and crowns, Have
3. Still let us sing the wondrous *grace* the sinner's debt that pays, The

song are ev - er sing - ing, full of prais - es, To
been on earth, for Je - sus, val - iant sol - diers; Their
Blood, too, that from ev - 'ry stain re - leas - es, The

Him whose Blood on Cal - va - ry for them in love was giv'n The
fight is o'er, death's stream they've cross'd, but still in heav'n resounds The
pow'r that spotless keeps the heart, while fill-ing it with praise, So

Blood by which was purchased their Sal - va - - tion.
song a - bout the Blood of their Re - deem - - er.
let us sing the song of Full Sal - va - - tion.

The Song of the Ages.

Praise, oh, praise Him! Swell the song that rang throughout the a - ges, Praise, oh, praise Him! The Lamb once slain! Oh, sing the grand old song a - gain, How the precious flow washes white as snow; Oh, sing the grand old song a-gain, Of the Fountain that was opened at the Cross.

Accompaniments in 8ves.

(87)

Grace Enough.

Words and Music by CAPTAIN H. EBBS.

mf Andante.

1. There's grace e - nough for all who to the Sav - iour go, Tho'
2. Thou'st sought be - fore? but didst thou seek by sav - ing faith? Tho'
3. Will dark days come? they may, and drear thy path may seem, But

bur - den'd with doubts and with fears; No long - er spurn His
fail - ure has brought grief and pain — For peace, for rest, for
then Christ the Lord goes be - fore, And He for all thy

grace; though spurned for years !
par - don try a - gain !
needs has grace in store.

mp CHORUS. *Allegretto.*

Grace for the wea - ry, In sin's path so drea - ry,
He now is near thee, Near to bless and keep thee,

Grace Enough.

1.

Is found in Je - sus, the might - y to save;......

2.

Come and fol - low Je - sus, for thee life He gave......

Chorus.

Words and Music by H. ANDERSON.

Oh, I'm glad I came to Je - sus, for He took my sins a - way, And He

washed me in His all - a - ton - ing Blood, He has giv - en new de - si - res, And with

cour-age me in - spires. As I tread the nar-row way that leads to God.

60. Haste Away to Jesus.

Words and Music by BANDMASTER HILL.

1. The An-gel of the Lord shall stand, While thousand thunders roar,
2. In vain they'll cry for rocks to hide Them from Je-ho-vah's face;
3. When once the Judgment-day is past, 'Twill be in vain to pray;

And swear by Heav'ns e-ter-nal Throne That time shall be no more;
But, cursed by sin, they'll be denied—They'll have no hid-ing-place;
Wher-ev-er then your lot is cast, For-ev-er you must stay,

The earth and ev-'ry-thing therein Shall melt with fer-vent heat,
Be-fore God's bar we all must go, And hear the sen-tence giv'n,
Oh! awful thought, when time's no more This is God's firm de-cree,

And sin-ners wail-ing in their sins Will have their God to meet.
"De-part, ye cur-sed, in-to Hell;" Or Come with Me to Heav'n."
In hap-pi-ness or woe you'll dwell Thro' all e-ter-ni-ty.

Haste Away to Jesus.

Chorus.

Haste a - way to Je - sus, Oh, hear the warn-ing cry;

Haste a-way

Haste a - way to Je - sus For death is draw-ing nigh.

Haste a-way

Chorus.

Words by F. W. FRY.

ff

On to con-quer we are march - ing, Lead-ing sin-ners to the

mf

Blood, Till our Flag unfurl'd shall be o - ver ev - 'ry land and sea,

f

And each na - tion own Je - ho - vah as their God.

61.

There Flows a Stream.

Words and Music by Major R. Slater.

1. There flows a stream from my riv - en side, Tender - ly the Lord is speak-ing;
2. "Your will a throne will you yield to me? Tender - ly the Lord is speak-ing;

For sin-stained hearts is the cleans-ing tide, Will you heed the gracious words?
"As King am I o'er your soul to be? Will you heed the gracious words?

The precious blood is flow-ing o'er my heart; It is cleansing, it is cleansing Be-

fore its waves my sin and fear de-part; It is flow-ing o'er my heart.

3 " My peace I give, it shall guard your heart;
  " My presence ne'er shall from you depart.

4 " Upon your heart I my laws will write,
  " Your darkened soul I will fill with light.

5 " I trod a path thorn-strewn for thee;
  " The cross-bound way will you tread for me?

6 " In love my life was laid down for thee;
  " A sin cleansed heart will you give to me?"

(92)

62.

Take it All.

Words and Music by COMMANDER BOOTH TUCKER.

p Andante.

1. Ac - cept my youth, my strength, my prime, Ac - cept each mo - ment
Earth's choicest joys I sac - ri - fice, And choose Thy smile at

D. C. CHORUS. *mf*

of   my time;
a - ny price.   } I hear and now o - bey the call, And

leap by faith, doubt's high - est wall;   I   can - not give Thee

less than all,   Take it   all,   Lord, take it   all!

2 Whate'er is wrong I here confess,
  Whate'er is good do Thou possess;
  Whatever seemeth to be mine,
  Oh make it Thine, Lord,—make it Thine!

CHO.—My life, my influence I bring,
  My treasures at Thy feet I fling,
  And crown Thee everlasting King,
  Heart and soul, Lord,—heart and soul.

3 My will, my mind, my heart inspire
  With more than pentecostal fire;
  Destroy the dross,—the self, the shame,
  In love's pure sin-consuming flame!

CHO.—Into the regions of despair,
  Into the midst of Satan's lair,—
  For dying soul's to do and dare,—
  Send me there, Lord, send me there.

4 Oh, hearken to our world wide plea,—
  God bless our world wide Jubilee!
  Deluge us with Salvation's flood!
  God speed the Flag of Fire and Blood!

CHO.—In Power Divine upon us fall!
  To save the world from Satan's thrall,
  We march obedient to Thy call,
  One and all, Lord,—one and all!

(93)

63. Ye Must Be Born Again.

Words and Music by BANDMASTER G. S. SMITH.

p Moderato.

1. When Je - sus was up-on the earth, One night a Ru-ler to Him came,
2. Oh, there are ma-ny liv-ing now Who real-ly can-not un-der-stand,
3. But that is not the Saviour's plan, He says, you must be born a-gain,
4. Your life will then become quite new, De - sires and motives will be pure;

cres.

Christ told him of a sec-ond birth, He said, "Ye must be born a-gain."
How 'tis that they can nev-er grow To be a follower of the Lamb.
And grace must kill the e-vil man That doth in human nature reign.
The world will lose its charms for you, You'll want its empty joys no more.

mf

The Rul-er could not understand How such a change could ever be,
They see not why they can't arrange To give up do-ing that or this,
Re-pent-ing of a life of sin, Cast-ing your all at Je-sus' feet,
Thus you will live a life di-vine, And spread abroad the Saviour's fame,

dim.

The Saviour's great sal-va-tion plan To him seem'd a great mystery.
And so ef-fect a graceful change, And en-ter in-to per-fect bliss
Be-liev-ing, He will take you in, And make your peace and joy complete.
Your light will ev-er bright-ly shine When you are real-ly born a-gain.

Ye Must Be Born Again.

f CHORUS.

Born a - gain, born a - gain, Je - sus
Born a - gain, born a - gain,

said, "Ye must be born a - gain;" Would you
born a - gain;"

en - ter the king-dom of heav-en, Ye must be born a - gain.

64. All I Have I am Bringing to Thee.

mp Andante.   Words and Music by COMMANDANT H. H. BOOTH.

1. All I have by Thy Blood Thou dost claim, Bless - ed
2. With my all at Thy cross, Lord, I part, See, I
3. All I have— it shall be noth - ing less.— All I

cres.

Lord, who for me once was slain; Now Thine own I will give Thee,
bring Thee my mind and my heart; Here's my bod - y and spir - it,
have Thou shalt own, Lord, and bless; Loss and pain shall not hin - der;

(95)

All I Have I am Bringing to Thee.

mf   *dim.* •

I know Thou wilt take me Tho' long Thou hast pleaded in vain.
My all Thou shalt have it, I'll live for Thy glo-ry a - lone.
I'll keep back no long-er, My all I now give Thee, my Lord.

mf CHORUS.

All I have I am bring-ing to Thee, All I

have I am bring-ing to Thee, In Thy steps I will fol-low,

Come joy or come sor-row, Dear Sav-iour, I will fol-low Thee.

4 Days of darkness there may be for me,
Rough and steep, too, my pathway may
    But the joy or the sorrow   [be;
    That comes with to-morrow,
Will just be the fittest for me.

5 Though by darkness my future is veiled,
Here's my all, for Thy love has prevailed;
    I no longer will doubt Thee,
    I know Thou dost take me,
My life shall be wholly for Thee.

65. A Friend Ever Faithful.

Words and Music by MAJOR R. SLATER.

1. I have a friend in whom I find rest; With peace un-brok - en
2. He in my sor - row brings me re - lief; His love as - sua - ges
3. All that I think and feel He doth know; Marked by His hand my
4. Death now for me pos sess - es no sting, Nor can the grave a

I am blest; Doubt-ing and fear no long - er mo-lest— But
all my grief; Calm is my rest - ing, for me be - neath His
path be - low, All will be well, come joy or come woe— For
vic - t'ry win; Safe, me to heav'n, my Sav-iour will bring, Tho'

CHORUS.

joy born of heav - en is mine
arms ev - er - lest - ing are held.
mine are His wis - dom and love...
dark and storm-beat-en my way....

A Friend ev - er faith-ful is

Je - sus my Sav-iour, For in His love He nev-er doth wav-er; And as in

joy, I've in sor - row His fav - our—Je - sus for ev - er is mine.

D   (97)

66. Never Quit the Field.

Words and Music by BLIND MARK.

1. Will you quit the field? Will you ev-er yield? Nev-er, nev-er,
2. When the foe is near Will you have a fear? Nev-er, nev-er,
3. Will you cease to sing Prais-es to your King? Nev-er, nev-er,

nev - er! Will you bold-ly fight And de-fend the right?
nev - er! Will you take your stand With faith's sword in hand?
nev - er! Brave-ly ev-'ry day Will you march a - way?

Yes, for - ev - er! Nev-er quit the field till the

foe is slain, Nev-er quit the field, oh, nev-er, nev - er yield;

Nev-er quit the field till we vic-t'ry gain, Nev-er, nev-er, nev - er!

67.

Come Home To-night.

F. E. HIMANOCZY.

Slow with expression.

1. If you lis - ten you will hear a voice......... That will make your ve-ry soul re - - joice—........ { "Son, I have purchased thee "Son, I have purchased thee
2. Ma - ny wea - ry years have pass'd since first you heard........ Of that wondrous love re-cord-ed in His Word;.......... { Love that still calls to thee Love that still calls to thee

Sal - va - tion rich and free; I wait to welcome thee, Come home to-night."
Sal - va - tion rich and free; I wait to welcome thee,
"Son, I have purchased thee Sal - va - tion rich and free, Come home to-night."
"Son, I have purchased thee Sal - va - tion rich and free,

Ritard. CHORUS. *Allegro.*

Come home to-night, For the an - gels are sweetly sing-ing, " Come home to-night; "

All the hosts of Heav'n swell,That chorus loud and bright— All the hosts of

(99)

Come Home To-night.

Ritard.

Heaven swell, That chorus loud and bright—"O sinner, come home to-night."

3 Listen now to mercy's voice, and then obey,
  Do not wait until a more convenient day,
    Time is fast fleeting by,
    Judgment is drawing nigh;
    Do not your God defy,
    Come home to-night.

4 Soon the Judgment Day will dawn and you shall stand
  In the presence of the King, at His command;
    Verdict you then shall hear,
    But you need have no fear,
    Jesus will save you here,
    Come home to-night.

68. The way of Light.

Words by MAJOR SLATER.   Music by Mrs. HOUGHTON.

mf Allegro Moderato.

1. There is a way that we may walk, Hav-ing as our Com-pan-ion
2. That is the way that bright-er shines, For those who for-ward jour-ney;
Cho.—I'll tread the way that love makes bright, Christ shall be my com-pan-ion,

Je-sus, and In lov-ing talk There is sweet com-mun-ion;
Straight it is and steep at times, But when the feet grow wea-ry,
In the war for truth and right, I will fol-low Je-sus;

The Way of Light.

Who are the souls that tread that way? Those who from sin are sev - ered,
Vis - ions of glo - ry on be - fore, Sights of the Gold-en Cit - y,
I'll tread the way that love makes bright; Christ shall be my Com - pan - ion,

FINE.

And the voice of God o - bey, His will their de - light.
Cheer the heart, of strength a store Is gained from the view.
In the war for truth and right, I'll fol - low my King.

Hal - le - lu - jah! Hal - le - lu - jah! Grand is the life that's lived for God!

Hal - le - lu - jah! Hal - le - lu - jah! By His grace kept good: Oh,

D. C. for Cho.

Sing - ing songs of praise for tri - umphs Won by the Blood.

69.

The Absent Guest.

Words by MAJOR SLATER.   Music by BANDMASTER APPLEBY.

mp Adagio.

1. For our sal - va - tion Je - sus paid a wondrous price,
2. Love's ten - der plead - ings, are they all to be in vain?
3. His com - ing hin - dered— Oh, how rest - less you have been!
4. Self serve no lon - ger— peace and joy sur - ren - der brings,

cres.

No tears of sor - row e'er for guilt could suf - fice;
Un - moved the bar - riers, will you still slight His claim,
Dark - ness a - round you, fears dis - tress - ing with - in,
Doubt - ing means bon - dage, faith springs as eagle's wings

mf rit.   *Allegro Moderato.*

To save the lost, what was the cost? A spot - less
Who, lov - ing true, gave all for you? A spot - less
A spir - it sore, with bolt - ed door! A spot - less
That glad - ly rise in sun - lit skies. The spot - less

cres.

Lamb, Himself He gave, By pi - ty mov'd, He died to save, Yet Christ your
Lamb, Himself He gave, By pi - ty mov'd, He died to save, Yet Christ your
Lamb, Himself He gave, By pi - ty mov'd, He died to save, Yet Christ your
Lamb, the one who gave Himself to death, your soul to save, Is stand - ing

The Absent Guest.

Lord, of friends, the best, Is from your soul an ab-sent guest, But
Lord, of friends, the best, Is from your soul an ab-sent guest, But
Lord, of friends, the best, Is from your soul an ab-sent guest, But
near, you may be blest, Your ransomed soul has not its guest, But

CHORUS. *Tempo di marcia.*

why? Swing open your heart's door to the Sav - iour, Bid Him

en - ter, dwell for - ev - er there, Swing o - pen your

heart's door to the Sav - iour, There let Him reign a - lone!

(103)

70.

Enlist in the Army.

L. E. Jones.   Jno. R. Bryant.

1. See our grand and no-ble ar - my that is marching on to-day; They are
2. See our grand and no-ble ar - my, and the Sav-iour leads the way As they're
3. In this grand and no-ble ar - my there is room for ma - ny more, And the
4. Then when fighting here is o - ver, and life's conflicts we have won, We will

march-ing 'neath the ban - ner of the Lord; Hear the cry that's ev - er
march-ing o'er the bat - tle - field of life; Tho' the foe may sore as-
call for new re - cruits we'll ev - er ring; In the ranks, oh, come en-
hear our Great Command-er's voice so true: "Lay a - side your dust-y

ringing, "Be ye rea - dy for the fray," Let us ral - ly quick-ly at His word.
sail them They shall never be dismayed, But shall ever con-quer in the strife.
list and put the shin-ing ar - mor on, Ev - er serv-ing faithful - ly the King.
ar - mor, come and wear the victor's crown, Pass before me in the grand re-view."

CHORUS.

En-list in the army, en - list in the army There's need of valiant soldiers true!

En-list in the army, en - list in the army, There waits a ready place for you.

71.

When the Pearly Gates Unfold.

mp Andante.

1. I have giv'n up all for Je - sus, This vain world is nought to me, All its
2. When the voice of Je - sus calls me, And the an - gels whis-per low, I will
3. Just be - yond the waves of Jor-dan, Just be-yond its chill- ing tide Blooms the

mf

pleasures are for - gotten In re-mem-b'ring Calva - ry ; Tho' my friends despise, for
lean up-on my Sav-iour, Through the val ley as I go ; I will claim His precious
tree of life im - mortal, And the liv - ing wa-ters glide ; In that hap-py land of

sake me, And on me the world looks cold, I've a Friend that will stand by me When the
promise, Worth to me the world of gold, "Fear no ev - il, I'll be with thee When the
spir- it, Flow-ers bloom on hills of gold, And the an - gels are a- wait - ing Where the

f CHORUS.

pear - ly gates un- fold." Life's morn will soon be waning, And the eve-ning bells will

toll ; But my heart will know no sad - ness When the pear - ly gates un - fold.

(105)

72.

'Twas In An Army Barracks.

Words by MAJOR LUDGATE.   TUNE:—" Just tell them that you saw me."

1. 'Twas in an Ar-my bar-racks in a dis-tant Western town, The
2. His moth-er got the let-ter as she lay at death's dark door, That

meet-ing there one night had just be-gun,   When in came a poor
told her of her boy so far a-way;   How his sins they were

drunkard who by sin had been bro't down, Thinking, perhaps, that he m'ght have some
forgiven, and his wand'ring days were o'er, And that his feet were on the nar-rov

fun.   But as he heard of Je-sus' love and pardon free for all, He
way.   Her heart was fill'd with gladness as it had not been for years, Her

By kind permission of W. Paul Dresser.

'Twas In An Army Barracks.

sought it and the wand'rer ceased to roam; And going to his room that night, his
dear old face was all lit up with joy, As up-on her dy-ing pillow she

heart all fill'd with joy, He sent a mes-sage to the folks at home.
said, a-mid her tears, "God bless and keep my precious darling boy."

p Chorus.

Just tell my dear old moth-er that my wand'ring days are o'er, Just

tell her that my sins are all for-giv'n; Just tell her that if we should chance on

rit

earth to meet no more, Her pray'rs are answer'd, and we'll meet in heav'n.

73.

Begone, Vain World.

1. Be - gone, vain world, thou hast no charms for me.
   My cap - tive soul has long been held by thee;
2. What are thy charms, could I com - mand the whole?
   Thy min - gled sweets could nev - er feed the soul,
3. My soul, thro' grace, on wings of faith shall rise
   T'ward that dear place where my pos - ses - sion lies;

I lis - tened long to thy vain song, And thought thy music sweet,
A no - bler prize at-tracts mine eyes, Where trees immor-tal grow,
That sa - cred land, at God's right hand, My dear Re-deem - er's throne.

And thus my soul lay grovel-ing at thy feet.
A fruit - ful land where milk and hon - ey flow.
Where Je - sus pleads, and makes my cause His own.

74.

The Banner of Calvary.

Tune—"The Star-Spangled Banner."   Words by Commander Booth Tucker

1. Have you heard the sweet sto-ry of Cal - va-ry's Cross, Of a Sav-iour who
   suffered and bled, how He counted all loss, Shedding blood-drops of

The Banner of Calvary.

died to ob·tain for us pardon—How He
grief in Geth·se·ma·ne's garden
Have you ever seen
how the thorns pierced His pale brow, Have you cried to Him ev·er "Lord
save me just now?" Does the banner of Cal·va·ry o·ver you
wave? Have you tast·ed the pow·er of Je·sus to save?

2 Oh, the banner of Calvary floats o'er the world !
   Tens of thousands gain hope as they hear its sweet flutter !
For it tells of a day when sin shall be down-hurled,
   Of a day whose bright joy mortal tongue cannot utter,
Of a day of new birth, when across the whole earth,
   All creation shall burst into singing and mirth !

Cho.—When the banner of Calvary o'er the world waves,
   And its nations shall cry in one day " Jesus saves."

3 Hallelujah ! That banner waves over my soul '
   Hallelujah ! Beneath its blest folds I am fighting !
Through the Blood of the Lamb I am saved and kept whole,
   In the fire of the Holy Ghost daily delighting !
And the banner still waves, while my glad spirit craves
   Nothing more than to shout through the world, Jesus saves !

Cho.—'Tis the Blood-and-Fire banner that through the world waves,
   And proclaims to the nations of earth, Jesus saves !

(109)

75.

Jesus Is Strong to Deliver.

Words and Music by Commandant H. H. Booth.

mp Allegretto.

1. Why are you doubting and fearing? Why are you still un-der sin?
2. You say, "I am weak, am helpless; I've tried a-gain and a-gain!"
3. When in my sor-row He found me, Found me, and bade me be whole,
4. When in the tem-pest He hides me, When in the storm He is near,

Have you not found, That His grace doth abound? He's mighty to save let Him in!
Well, this may be true But 'tis not what you do—'Tis He who's the mighty to save!
Turned all my night Into heavenly light, And from me my burden did roll!
All the way 'long He carries me on, Now I have noth-ing to fear

f Chorus.

Je-sus is strong to de-liv-er! Might-y to save! mighty to save!

Je-sus is strong to de-liv-er! Je-sus is might-y to save!

Oh, What Battles I've Been In.

Words by COMMANDANT H. H. BOOTH.

1. { Oh, what battles I've been in, And what con-flicts I have seen,
   { Oh, what mocking and what shame I can suf-fer for His name,

But in dark-ness as in bright-ness, He is mine!

For in glo-ry as the stars He'll make me shine.

CHORUS.

Wash'd in the Blood white as snow, Nothing am I seeking here be-low;

There's no more strife for my soul I know, And nought can my peace overthrow.

2 What a sinner I have been,
What a Saviour I have seen,
For He saved me from my sorrow and my woe!
And when lost to all around,
My Redeemer then I found,
And His pard'ning love and mercy now I know.

3 Oh, what mighty wondrous love.
Brought my Saviour from above,
On the Cross to shed His blood and die for me !
Oh, I'll serve Him with my might,
In His service I'll delight,
For the Blood from sin's dark bondage sets me free.

(111).

77. My Heart's Door Wide I'm Swinging.

Words of verses by MAJOR LUDGATE. TUNE:—"Just break the news to mother."

1. There is full and free sal-va-tion for ev-'ry burdened soul
2. Ma-ny years I spent in fol-ly and trampled on God's love,
3. 'Tis the prom-ise of the Fa-ther, re-cord-ed in His Word,

Who will come to Calvary's Riv-er and be made ful-ly whole.
Was stub-born and re-bel-lious and turned from God a-bove;
To give a full sal-va-tion, to Him you are re-ferred;

From the stains of sin it cleanses, and brings sweet joy and peace,
But the lov-ing Sav-iour found me, and wooed and won my heart,
If in full, com-plete sub-mis-sion you seek to do His will,

From ev-'ry sin-ful pas-sion there's re-lease. Many times I've proved its
And promised He from me would nev-er part. Then a full and free sur-
The Ho-ly Spir-it all your heart will fill. All the chains of sin He'll

My Heart's Door Wide I'm Swinging.

pow-er, and to-day I feel and know The precious Blood it cleanses white as
ren-der to His will I there did make; I yield-ed ev-'ry a-tom of my
sev-er, ev-'ry barrier He'll remove, In place of un-be-lief there will be

snow. Hal-le-lu-jah for the Riv-er which flows for ev-'ry soul! Praise
will. Now I'm His to do or suf-fer, for joy or grief or woe, Wher-
love. Oh, this won-der-ful sal-va-tion that flows from Calv'ry's tide, Was

CHORUS.

God, I know it makes me fully whole!
e'er His Spir-it leads me I will go.   My heart's door wide I'm swinging, My
o-pened by a spear in Jes-us' side.

all to Thee I'm bringing, For cleans-ing and for pow-er I am

coming, Lord, to Thee! My pow-er I am coming, Lord, to Thee!

Mighty to Keep.

Words and Music by COMMANDANT H. H. BOOTH.

p Andante con espress.

1. Sometimes I'm tried with toil and care, Sometimes I'm weak and worn,
2. Nev-er I've known a cloud so dark, Nev-er a pow'r so strong,
3. Je-sus, I'll trust Thee more and more, Trust where I can-not trace,

Sometimes it looks so dark ev-'ry-where, Instead of the rose, the thorn.
Nev-er a wolf so fierce-ly to bark, Nev-er a night so long—
Trust when I hear the o-cean's roar, Trust when the foe I face.

These are the times, when tempted sore, A voice in my ear doth speak—
But they all vanished, and fell, and fled, And left me to wonder, not weep,
Thou wilt be more than life to me, So broad, so high, so deep,

"Unsheath thy sword, there's vict'ry before, Thy Saviour is mighty to keep."
How I could ever have doubted at all A Saviour so mighty to keep.
Chang-ing the thun-der in - to glee, A - ble to save and to keep.

Mighty to Keep.

mf CHORUS.

I have a Saviour who's mighty to keep, Mighty to keep, mighty to keep;

I have a Saviour who's mighty to keep, Mighty to keep ev-er-more.

79.

A Dream of the Judgment.

Words by a Captain in the United States.

1. I dream'd that the great Judgment morning Had dawn'd, and the trumpet had blown,
2. The rich man was there, but his money Had melted and vanished a-way,
3. The widow was there, and the orphan. God heard and remembered their cries,
4. The moral man came to the Judgment, But his self-righteous rags would not do;

I dream'd that the nations had gather'd In Judgment before the White Throne,
A pauper he stood at the Judg-ment, His debts were too heavy to pay.
No sor-row in Heaven, for-ev-er, God wiped all the tears from their eyes.
The men that had crucified Je-sus, They passed off as moral men too.

(115)

A Dream of the Judgment.

From the Throne went a bright shining angel, And stood on the land and the sea,
The great man stood there but his greatness When death came was left far behind.
The gambler was there, and the drunkard, And the man that had sold him the drink,
The souls that had put off salvation—"Not to-night, I'll get saved by-and bye,

And swore, with his Hand rais'd to heaven, That Time was no longer to be,
The an-gel that car-ried the rec-ords No trace of his greatness could find.
With the people who gave him the license, To-geth-er in hell they did sink.
No time now to think of re-lig-ion"—At last they had found time to die.

And swore, with his hand rais'd to heaven, That Time was no longer to be.
The an-gel that car-ried the rec-ords No trace of his greatness could find.
With the people who gave him the license, To-geth-er in hell they did sink.
No time now to think of re-lig-ion"—At last they had found time to die.

mf Chorus.

Then, oh, what a weeping and wailing, When the lost ones heard of their fate!

They cried to the rocks and the mountains, They pray'd, but their pray'r was too la'e!

80.

God be With You.

J. E. RANKIN, D.D.

W. G. TOMER.   By per.

1. God be with you till we meet a- gain, By His counsels guide uphold you,
2. God be with you till we meet a- gain, 'Neath His wings securely hide you,
3. God be with you till we meet a- gain, When life's perils thick confound you,
4. God be with you till we meet a- gain, Keep love's banner floating o'er you,

With His sheep se cure-ly fold you,   God be with you till we meet again.
Dai - ly man- na still pro-vide you,   God be with you till we meet again.
Put His arms un-fail ing round you,   God be with you till we meet again.
Smite death's threat'ning wave before you, God be with you till we meet again.

REFRAIN.

Till we meet,   till we meet,   Till we meet at Je-sus' feet,

Till we meet, till we meet, till we meet, Till we meet at Jesus' feet, Till we meet,

Till we meet, ... till me meet,   . God be with you till we meet again.

Till we meet, till we meet, till we meet, God be with you till we meet a-gain.

The Golden City.

m.f. Allegro moderato

Words and Music by COMMANDANT H. H. BOOTH.

1. I've a home fair and bright in yon-der Cit - y, To its
2. It is true on the way to yon-der Cit - y, I've to
3. Do you know there's no place in yon-der Cit - y, For a

gates I am march-ing a - long; When my fight - ing for Je-sus here is
cross o'er a cold roll - ing flood; But I trust Him to guide me by whose
soul that is bur-dened with guilt? Do you know that no sin can ev-er

o - ver, I shall then take my place with the throng That
pi - ty I've been led to the sin - cleans- ing Blood; As
en - ter? Hast - en then to the Blood that was spilt To

face to face be - holds the Saviour, In whose praise is raised its song.
He has said He'll nev - er leave me, I will trust my Friend, my God.
cleanse from sin, and with me jour ney To the Cit - y God has built.

f CHORUS.

Up in the golden Cit - y There's a mansion to me will be giv'n; I am

The Golden City.

rich - er by far Than a Queen or a Czar, I'm an heir of the wealth of heav'n.

82.

A Never-failing Friend.

Words and Music by COMMANDANT H. H. BOOTH.

mp Andante.

1. { A Friend I have found who my needs hath sup-plied, A Friend who my
   { A Friend who no bless-ing my soul hath de-nied, Nor suf-fered my

sor - row hath soothed. } He smiles! I am blest, He rules! I have
heart to be moved.

rest, His pres-ence destroys ev - 'ry fear;...... How can I be

ev- er by sor-row oppress'd, With Jesus my spir- it to cheer......

[119]

A Never-failing Friend.

f CHORUS. *Allegretto.*

A nev - er - fail - ing Friend! A nev - er - fail - ing Friend! Is

Christ to me, So rich and free, His fa - vors nev - er end, A

nev - er - fail - ing Friend! A nev - er - fail - ing Friend! Give

up your sin, And you shall win A nev - er - fail - ing Friend.

2 This Friend I have found no respector is He
    All classes with Him are the same;
  The poor and the rich, and the bond and the free,
    His mercy and pardon may claim.
  I sought, He was near; I prayed, He did hear;
    I proved that He loved even me;
  I rose from the tomb of my sorrow and fear,
    And claimed Him my Saviour to be.

3 A Friend I have found who has taught me the charm
    Of loving the purest and best,
  And into the wounds of my heart poured the balm
    Of healing, and comfort, and rest;
  His pain brings renown, His Cross brings the crown,
    To serve Him is now my one care;
  And here at His Cross I have laid myself down,
    And trust to be kept ever there.

83.

Love Divine.

Tune : " Calcutta."

1. Love di-vine from Je-sus flow-ing Liv-ing wa-ters, rich and free,
2. Love sur-pass-ing un-der-stand-ing, An-gels would the mys-tery scan,
3. Love that par-dons past transgression, Love that cleanses ev-'ry stain,
4. From my soul break ev-'ry fet-ter, Thee to know is all my cry;

Wondrous love, with-out a lim-it, Flow-ing thro' e - ter-ni-ty.
Yet so ten-der that it reach-es To the low-est child of man.
Love that fills to o-ver-flow-ing, And in-vites to drink a-gain!
Sa-viour, I am thine for-ev-er, Thine, I'll live, and Thine I'll die.

CHORUS.

Boundless ocean, boundless ocean, I would cast myself on Thee, I would cast myself on Thee, I would
Let me, Je-sus, let me. Je-sus, Better know salvation's plan, Better know salvation's plan, Bet ter
Precious fountain, precious fountain! Which to open Christ was slain, Which to open Christ was slain, Which to
On - ly asking, only asking, More and more of love's supply, More and more of love's supply, More and

cast my-self on Thee, ...   I would cast myself on Thee.
know sal-va-tion's plan, ...   Better know salvation's plan.
o - pen Christ was slain, ...   Which to open Christ was slain.
more of love's sup-ply, ...   More and more of love's supply.

My Home is in Heaven.

1. I have a home that is fair-er than day, And my dear
2. Friends, I shall see, who have jour-neyed be-fore, And land-ed
3. Oh, who will jour-ney to heav-en with me? Je-sus has

Sa-viour has shown me the way; Oft when I'm sad and temp-
safe on that beau-ti-ful shore; I shall see Je-sus, that
died that we all may go free; Come, then, to Him who has

ta-tions a-rise, I look to my home far a-way.
will be my joy. In that bright home far, far a-way.
pur-chased for Thee, A crown in that home far a-way.

CHORUS.

My home is in heaven, there is no part-ing there, All will be hap-py,

glo-rious bright and fair; There will be no sor-row

My Home is in Heaven.

there will be no tears, In that bright home far a - way.

85.

Oh, What a Redeemer.

Words and Music by COMMANDANT H. H. BOOTH.

1. Re-deem - ing grace! my life has claim-ed, That it from hence may
2. Re-deem - ing grace! my life is giv - en, For such a prize as
3. Re-deem - ing grace! my all is laid Be - fore the Cross of

be, For ev - er God's by sin unstained, In glo-rious lib - er -
this; The pow'r of love my heart is riv'n, And filled with fade-less
Him, Whose life and death a means were made, My wayward heart to

ty. What charms of earth, can e'er, The pitying love defy Him
bliss. What joys of time can hope, Tho' decked with blossoms fair, With-
win, Oh, let my ev'ry act, Breathe, Lord, a praise to Thee; And

Oh, What a Redeemer.

who laid His glo - ry by, And came for me to die?
in my heart the fa - vor claimed, By God-giv'n joys to share?
let my life be lived to show How cap - tives may be free.

mf CHORUS, *Allegretto moderato.*

Oh, what a Re - deem - er is Je - sus my

Sav - iour! For - giv-ing my sins, ... And

bear - ing all my woe. . . . . . Pro - claim-ing my

lib - er - ty, And wash-ing me white as snow. . . . .

(124)

Give Me the Faith.

TUNE:—Stella.

_f_

1. { Give me the faith that Je - sus had, The faith that can great
   { That makes the mourn-ful spir - it glad, The sav - ing

2. { Give me the faith that gets the pow'r, That stubborn dev - ils
   { That li - on-teeth can - not de - vour, That fur - nace

3. { Give me the faith that dare do right, That keeps the weak - est
   { That will for Je - sus no - bly fight, That turns life's

_pp_

moun - tains move, faith that works by love; The faith for
can not turn, fires can nev - er burn; That nev - er
brave and strong, sor - rows in - to song, That pass - es

which the saints have striv'n, The faith that pulls the fire from heav'n.
fears the ty - rant's frown, That wins and wears the mar- tyr's crown.
through the fie - ry test, That lives and gives and does the best.

CHORUS. _Quicker._

{ Oh, the blood of Je - sus, The precious blood of Je - sus,
{ Oh, the blood of Je - sus, It clean-ses from all sin.

To the War!

Words and Music by COMMANDER BOOTH TUCKER.

mf Allegro moderato.

1. To the War, to the War! let us mar - shall our le gious! Let
2. To the War, to the War! by his fu - ri - ous driv ing Let
3. Let each sin that hath reign'd with our ar - rows be smitten, Let
4. To the War, to the War! let no ling - er - er tar - ry, Or

ho - ly am-bi - tion our spir-it inspire! Let us claim for our King the earth's
each Captain Je-hu from far become known! Let each Soldier and Sergeant, for
Je - ze-bel pleasures be flung from the wall! Let Salvation across the world's
an-swer, 'This trumpet-call is not for me;' The good tid-ings of mer - cy the

ut - ter-most regions, And march to the res-cue with Blood and with Fire!
vic - to - ry striving, Join hands till the dev - il from earth we de-throne!
sad heart be writ-ten, And Je - sus Je - ho - vah be King o - ver all!
weak - est may car - ry, There's room for the world in love's fath-omless sea!

f CHORUS.

To the War, to the War! Wave the Flag, beat the Drum! To the

To the War!

War, to the War! Till Christ's Kingdom shall come! To the War! Bid the nations behold their "Desire!" To the War, to the War, with the Blood and the Fire!

88. Then Hoist the Flag of Liberty.

Words by ADJ. E. TUCKER.

Music by STAFF CAPT. OSTBY, (Norway.)

mf Andantino.

1. In bat - tle heat or peace serene, In storm or calm the same, Our
2. The sol-dier brave, cares not to save His life at oth - ers' risk, The
3. With joy we forward march, and take, To ev-'ry slave of sin E -

Lead - er King, He reigns supreme, E - man-uel is His name. When
vic - t'ry gained o'er death and grave, No long - er can he list To
man - ci - pa - tion, ere to late. Thro' Je-sus Christ our King, From

Then Hoist the Flag of Liberty.

tired and wea - ry in the fray, Dis couraged, not cast down, A
Sa-tans' smooth but hell - ish words Of com - fort, ease and rest, But
bond-age lib - er - ty there is; This glo-rious news is true. O

voice comes from the van, "O-bey, En-dure, and win the crown!"
down where sin and sor - row lurks, He fights, there he's most blest.
sin - ner, come, for grace like this Our Sav-iour of - fers you.

CHORUS.
ff Vivace.

Then hoist the flag of lib - er-ty, The glo - rious Blood and Fire, Till

Marcato.

ev - 'ry na - tion, saved and free, Its mot - to shall in - spire.

(128)

89.

Win It?

Words and Music by Staff Captain T. H. Adams.

1. For - ward march, ye war - riors of the Cross, Count-ing all this
2. Man - y things will come to mar your peace, But His Grace will
3. When you're tempt-ed to for-sake your God, Keep straight on the
4. Raise the Stand - ard, yel - low, red and blue, To its sym - bols

world but dung and dross; Liv - ing al - ways close be-side the Cross,
bring you sure re-lease, And your strength each moment will in - crease,
path your Sav - iour trod, He will bear your heav - y, heav - y load,
ev - er, ev - er true, To the front, ad - vance, to dare and do,

Chorus.

Serv - ing Christ your Lord. March on, we shall win the Day,

March on, we shall win the Day; Win it? Win it? Of

course we'll win it! We shall win the Day.

90.

On the Cross of Calvary.

1. On the Cross of Cal-va-ry Je-sus died for you and
2. Oh, what won-drous, wondrous love, Brought me down at Je-sus'
3. Take me, Je-sus, I am Thine, Whol-ly Thine, for ev-er-

me, There He shed His precious Blood, That from sin we might be
feet; Oh, such won-drous dy-ing love, Asks a sac-ri-fice com-
more; Bless-ed Je-sus, Thou art mine; Dwell with-in for-ev-er-

free, Oh, the cleans-ing stream does flow, And it washes white as snow,
plete. Here I give my-self to Thee, Soul and bod-y, Thine to be;
more. Cleanse, oh-cleanse, my heart from sin, Make and keep me pure with-in;

It was for me that Je-sus died On the Cross of Cal-va-ry.
It was for me Thy blood was shed On the Cross of Cal-va-ry.
It was for this Thy blood was shed On the Cross of Cal-va-ry.

(130)

On the Cross Of Calvary.

CHORUS.

Of Cal - va - ry,.............. Of Cal - va - ry,...............

Of Cal - va - ry, Of Cal - va - ry,

It was for me that Je - sus died On the Cross of Cal - va - ry.

91. There's a Laying Down of Crosses.

Words and Music by MAJOR R. SLATER.

1. We have each a cross to bear, As we fol - low Je - sus here,
2. In the path we have to tread Man - y wea - ry feet have bled
3. When dark clouds are o - ver head And no ray of light is shed
4. Let your mem - o - ry be stored With the prom - is - es of God,

And some hardships we as sol - diers must en - dure, But there's
As they've journeyed on the up - ward track to heav'n; Tho' there's
On the path you take for Je - sus, still hold on; Aft - er
So to keep a - way the doubts that else will come; Brave - ly

There's a Laying Down of Crosses.

com - ing on a time When we our cross - es shall re - sign As we're
sor - row, toil and pain For all who would the summit gain, Grace e -
all it is not long That for His sake the cross is borne, Soon by
toil and do your best., And dare to leave with God the rest, So march

mp Chorus.

called to the saints re-ward.
nough will by God be giv'n.
us will the crown be won.
on till you reach the Throne.

There's a lay-ing down of cross-es, And a

tak - ing up of crowns, There is free - dom from earth's losses, And the

care which here a-bounds, When we from this world shall sever, And we

get be-yond the riv-er, To our home to dwell for ev-er with our God.

92.

I'm Glad I'm Ready.

Words and Music by Commandant H. H. Booth.

1. There's a gold-en day, And 'tis not far a-way, When the Prince of all the
Then the hosts shall raise Loud their voices in praise, While with "Righteousness of

earth shall no longer delay, But shall send forth the call To the nations all For the
saints" the Bride herself ar-rays; And with rapturous song They will march along To the

CHORUS.

Royal Marriage Supper of the Lamb! Oh, I'm glad I'm ready! Oh, I'm glad I'm ready!
Royal Marriage Supper of the Lamb!

Ready with the "wedding garment" on! Fighting till I join the hap-py throng!

2 There's a Cross you must bear,
And a Robe you must wear,
If the glories of the Marriage Supper you
would share;
You must be quite sure
That for Him you'll endure
Till the Royal Marriage Supper of the Lamb!
There must not one stain
On your garment remain
If you wish to seek the favor of the Bride-
groom to gain!
For no sin shall enter in
To the Palace of the King
At the Royal Marriage Supper of the Lamb!

3 When the fighting's o'er,
And I reach the shore;
Where wickedness and misery shall be no
more!
With a joyful heart
I shall then take part
In the Royal Marriage of the Lamb!
To the Lamb that was slain,
Power and honor proclaim,
For o'er both earth and Heaven He has right
to reign!
Yet my heart is His throne,
And my life is His own;
Till to share the Marriage Supper I shall go!

(133)

93. Sweetness in the Blessing.

Words by S. H. HODGES.   TUNE:—On the banks of the Wabash.

1. Would you know the full - ness of the Gos-pel Bless-ing, Prove the
2. Un - der Heav'n no oth - er name but Christ's is giv - en, And no

rich - es of the King-dom here on earth ; Would you
oth - er way for bless-ing can be found; On the

be the pearl of greatest price possess-ing And en-joy the gifts which
pag - es of the scripture it is writ - ten, Those who trust in Him have

are of heav'n-ly worth. Then to the Cross bring all your earthly
built on sol - id ground. But trust in Him means true obedience

treas - ure, No more must it be ev - er called your own; And
ev - er, And wit-ness - es for Him we all must be; From

By kind permission of Mr. Paul Dresser.

(134)

Sweetness in the Blessing.

tell to all the world from it you sev - er, As a sol-dier in the
all un-righteousness our hearts must sever, Then the glo ry of His

CHORUS. *Espressivo.*

ranks of God be known.
king-dom we shall see.
Oh, there's sweetness and there's glory in the

bless - ing, For the sol - dier who the world has counted

dross; . . . . When to all a-round the Sav-iour He's con-

pp

fess - ing, In his heart shines a glo-ry from the Cross.

94.

Onward, Yes, Onward.

(SECULAR MELODY.)

Words by COMMANDANT H. H. BOOTH.

p Andante.

1. On-ward, yes, onward, does time in its flight   Bear you a - long to e -
2. On-ward, yes, onward, you're borne on sin's years Till you've grown weary of
3. Tired of the hol-low, the base, and un - true, Sin - ner, oh, sin - ner, 'tis
4. Backslider, backslider, the time has been long, Since last in your mouth was

p

ter - ni - ty's night; Sin-ner, when once on the   e - cho-less shore,
toil and   of tears, Toil with-out   re - com-pense, tears all in vain;
Je - sus calls you;   For ma - ny years your sor - row He has seen,
heard the new song: Come to the Cross, and a - gain it will seem

mf   *dim.*   *mf*

An-swers to pray-er will come nev-er more. Tear from your soul now he
Will you not come to your Fa - ther a - gain? You have grown weary of
God's righteous anger and you stood between. Yet with strong yearning, and
That your black-slidings are gone like a dream. Now, in re-pentance, come

f

dark de-mon's snare, Come to the Cross with your woe and de - spair,
things that de - cay— Wea - ry of fling-ing your soul's wealth a - way;
filled with sin's pain. His fa - vor and love you're longing to   gain,
back to the place Where, like the prod - i - gal, you shall find grace,

Onward, Yes, Onward.

Down at the feet of the Saviour, oh, cry, "Par-don the past, Saviour,
Wea-ry of sow-ing what soon you must reap. Je-sus will hear, sinner—
Come from your darkness, oh, now to Him cry, "Par-don the past, Saviour;
Speak, while in sor-row be-fore Him you lie: "Par-don the past, Saviour;

save, or I die. Par-don the past, Sav-iour, save, or I die."
speak, sin-ner speak! Je-sus will hear, sin-ner—speak, sinner, speak!
save, or I die. Par-don the past, Sav-iour; save, or I die."
save, or I die. Par-don the past, Sav-iour; save, or I die!"

CHORUS.

Then shall the waves of the wild tempest cease, For thro' Thy Blood, Saviour,

I shall find peace, For through Thy Blood, Saviour, I shall find peace.

(137)

95. The Saviour Chose a Lowly Place.

(A CHRISTMAS SONG.)

Words and Music by Major R. Slater.

Andante.

1. The Sav-iour chose a low-ly place, When He in Beth-le-hem was born:
2. He glad-ly left His heavenly home The er-ring steps of men to trace.
3. From loving hearts O let us bring To Him the gift of thank-ful praise;

'Twas but a man-ger— Oh, what grace To sin-ful men the Lord has shown!
Who, tho' oft warned, still wandered on Towards the gloom of hell's a-byss.
Think how He stooped at Beth-le-hem, And at the Cross displayed His grace.

Bend-ing low,............ Seek-ing so............ Men to

p dolce.

Bending low, Seek-ing so,

save .... from end-less loss,............ Christ came

Men to save from end-less loss, end-less loss,

down........ and left His Throne .... To give, etc.

cres.

Christ came down, And left His Throne To give His life up-on the Cross.

(138)

I'll Cling Closer to Jesus.

Words by F. CALVERT.

1. Looking oft un - to Je - sus, in Him I can see, A Friend ev-er
2. By look-ing to Je - sus I've left far be - hind The worldly de-
3. Looking oft un - to Je - sus, in faith I can see, A white robe in
4. Looking oft un - to Je - sus, oh, may I be found Still clinging to

faith - ful who will not leave me; My hand clasp-eth His, and He
sires that once filled my poor mind; My fear has all van ished, my
heav - en that there a - waits me; If I but prove faith-ful, and
Him when the might - y trump sounds; Then I in His pres-ence shall

walks by my side, And un - der His col - ors I'll fight till I die.
pride has all gone, And now I am marching to heav-en my home.
His word o - bey, A crown He will give me in heav-en one day.
ev - er - more be, But how will it be, sin - ner, when He calls thee?

CHORUS.

I'll cling clos - er to Je - sus, I'll cling clos - er to Him,

I'll cling clos - er to Je - sus, The might - y to save.

(139)

97. The Lord Will Be Gracious.

Words by MAJOR R. SLATER.   Music by BANDSMAN ALEX. EDWARDS.

Allegro con espress.

1. Oh, why long - er lin - ger, sin - ner, in thy sad - ness?
2. Though low thou hast fal - len, yet there's grace to help thee;
3. There's no one but Je - sus can to thee give heal - ing,

For all thy sor - row the Lord will change to glad - ness;
Though great thy sin, yet, the Lord will par - don free - ly;
Come then to Him, and, in pen - i - tence while kneel - ing,

He waits to for - give thee, oh, think not that thy bad - ness
Oh, come now and trust in the Lord's un - meas - ured mer - cy,
The light from the Cross shall fall on thy soul, re - veal - ing

Should keep thee from Je - sus, for sin - ners He died to save.
Thy bonds shall be brok - en, and Je - sus will set thee free.
The might of that Blood that thy Sav - iour has shed for thee.

(140)

The Lord Will Be Gracious

The Lord will be gra - cious to ev - e - ry pen - i - tent

heart, The Lord will be gra - cious, oh, sin - ner, come

just as thou art!.. .... The Lord will be gra - cious, to

Him bring thy bur - den of sin! Oh, seek His face and

take thy place At the Cross where He died for thee.....

A Charge to Keep I Have.

Words by CHARLES WESLEY.

1. A charge to keep I have, A God to glo-ri-fy,...... A
2. To serve the pres - ent age, My call-ing to ful-fill, ... My

God to glo - ri - fy. A nev-er, a nev-er,
call - ing to ful - fill. Oh, may it, oh, may it,

A nev-er,
Oh, may it,

a nev - er dy-ing soul to save, And fit it for the sky, And
oh may it all my pow'rs en-gage To do my Master's will! To

fit it for the
do my Master's

Repeat for Chorus.

fiit it for the sky, And fit ..... it for the sky.
do my Master's will. To do ..... my Mas-ter's will.

sky, for thy sky,
will, Mas-ter's will,

(142)

99. I'll Stand For Christ Alone.

Words and Music by F. W. FRY.

mp *Allegro moderato.*

1. In the Ar-my of Je-sus I've tak-en my stand, To fight 'gainst the forces of
2. We go forth not to fight 'gainst the sin-ner, but sin, The lost and the out-cast we
3. Je-sus pit-ied our race, and He died in our place, To save a lost world was He
4. Our war-fare is great and our en-e-my's strong, Our aim he will ev-er op-

cres.

sin, To the res-cue we go, Sa-tan's pow'r to o'er-throw, And his
love; The claims of our King be - fore them we bring, And we
slain; But He rose and now lives, and His par-don He gives Un-to
pose; But the bat-tle's the Lord's and to Him we be-long, And with

mf CHORUS.

cap-tives to Je-sus we'll win. I'll stand for Christ, For Christ a-
urge them His mer-cy to prove.
those who will call on His name. I'll stand for Christ,
Him we shall con-quer our foes,

lone, A - mid the tem - pest and the storm, Where Je-sus
for Christ a-lone, tem - pest, tempest and the storm.
A-mid the tempest,

I'll Stand For Christ Alone.

leads, I'll fol-low on, I'll stand, I'll stand for Christ a-lone.
Where Jesus leads. I'll fol-low on,

100. ## America.

(NATIONAL HYMN.)

HENRY CAREY.

1. My coun - try! 'tis of thee, Sweet land of lib - er - ty,
2. My na - tive coun - try thee, Land of the no - ble, free,
3. Let mu - sic swell the breeze, And ring from all the trees
4. Our fa - thers' God! to thee, Au - thor of lib - er - ty,

Of thee I sing: Land where my fa - thers died! Land of the
Thy name I love; I love thy rocks and rills, Thy woods and
Sweet freedom's song: Let mor - tal tongues a - wake; Let all that
To thee we sing: Long may our land be bright With free-dom's

pil-grims' pride! From ev - 'ry moun - tain side Let free-dom ring!
tem - pled hills: My heart with rap - ture thrills Like that a - bove.
breathe par-take; Let rocks thy si - lence break, The sound pro - long.
ho - ly light; Pro - tect us by thy might, Great God our King!

(144)

101

All Round the World.

Tune—"Old Black Joe." B. B. 47.
S. M. 1., 387. M. S., VI.,
97, 10s.

1. All round the world the Army
   chariot rolls,
All round the world the Lord is saving souls,
All round the world our soldiers will
   be brave;
Around our colors we will rally—
   wave, soldiers, wave.

CHORUS.

Keep waving, keep waving, keep every
   flag unfurled,
We soon shall have our colors waving
   all round the world.

2. All round the world with music and
   with song,
All round the world we'll boldly
   march along,
All round the world to free each sin-
   bound slave,
We'll wave our Army flags for Jesus—
   wave, soldiers, wave.

3. All round the world the Saviour's
   blood shall flow,
All round the world we will to battle
   go,
All round the world the universe to
   save,
With blood and fire, with faith and
   feeling—wave, soldiers, wave.

102

The Lily of the Valley.

BY BANDMASTER FRY.

P. M.

1. I've found a friend in Jesus, He's
   everything to me,
   He's the fairest of ten thousand to
      my soul:
The Lily of the Valley, in Him alone I
   see
      All I need to cleanse and make me
      fully whole;
In sorrow He's my comfort, in trouble
   He's my stay,
      He tells me every care on Him to
      roll.

CHORUS.

He's the Lily of the Valley,
The Bright and Morning Star,
He's the fairest of ten thousand to my
   soul.

2. He all my griefs has taken, and all
   my sorrows borne,
   In temptation He's my strong and
      mighty tower;
I've all for Him forsaken, I've all my
   idols torn
   From my heart, and now He keeps
   me by His power.
Though all the world forsake me, and
   Satan tempt me sore,
   Through Jesus I shall safely reach
   the goal.

3. He'll never never leave me, nor yet
   forsake me here,
   While I live by faith and do His
      blessed will;
A wall of fire about me, I've nothing
   now to fear;
   With His manna He my hungry soul
   shall fill;
Then sweeping up to Glory, I'll see
   His blessed face,
   Where rivers of delight shall ever
   flow.

103

Will You Go ?

Tune—"Eden Above." B. J. 5. S.
M., I., 254. 12s and 11s.

1. We're bound for the land of the
   pure and the holy,
   The home of the happy, the king-
      dom of love:
Ye wanderers from God, in the broad
   road of folly,
   Oh, say, will you go to the Eden
   above?

CHORUS.

Will you go, will you go, will you go,
   will you go?
Oh, say, will you go to the Eden
   above?

2. In that blessed land neither sighing
   nor anguish
Can breathe in the fields where the
   glorified rove:

Ye heart-burdened ones, who in
  misery languish,
  Oh, say, will you go to the Eden
  above?

3. Each saint has a mansion prepared
  and all furnished,
  Ere from this small house he is
  summoned to move;
Its gates and its towers with glory
  are burnished,
  Oh, say, will you go to the Eden
  above?

4. March on, happy soldiers, the land
  lies before you,
  And soon its ten thousand delights
  we shall prove;
  Yes, soon we'll be massed on the
  hills of bright glory,
  And drink the pure joys of the
  Eden above.

LAST CHORUS.

We will go, we will go, we will go,
  we will go—
Oh, yes, we will go to the Eden
  above!

104

If We Fight Then We Shall Win.

Tune—"When the Mists Have Rolled
  Away."

1. When the true Salvation soldiers
  Hear the trump of Gabriel sound,
Sounding forth like peals of thunder
  Standing both on sea and ground,
Crying, "Time shall be no longer—
Rise, and to your Saviour flee,
Come, ye blessed of my Father,
  Spend a grand eternity."

CHORUS.

If we fight then we shall win,
Driving all the powers of sin,
And go forward, never tiring,
  In the hallelujah way,
We shall ride up in the chariot
On the resurrection day.

2. Now, my comrades, still go for-
  ward,
  Push the battle to the gate.
Preach salvation to the outcast
  For the great Redeemer's sake;

Never slacking, never faltering,
Never dragging on behind,
Then success will crown our efforts
  In the saving of mankind.

3. Then with friends who've gone be-
  fore us
  And have reached the golden
  strand,
We shall join the joyful chorus
  As we stand before the Lamb,
Telling of the many blessings
  We've received from day to day,
And the glorious revelations
  That we've witnessed on the way.

105

Gone is My Burden.

1. Just from the fountain and now
  we can sing
  Happy oh, happy in Jesus;
Just from the brink of the life-giving
  spring,
  Happy, oh, happy in Jesus.

CHORUS.

Gone is my burden, He rolled it
  away;
Opened my eyes to the light of the
  day;
Now in the fullness of joy I can say,
  Happy, oh, happy in Jesus.

2. Just from the fountain—'twas sweet
  to be there.
  Saved through the merits of Jesus;
Asking the aid of His Spirit in prayer,
  Holding communion with Jesus.

3. Just from the fountain of mercy
  are we.
  Happy, oh, happy in Jesus;
Sinner, the fountain is flowing for
  thee,
  Come in, be happy in Jesus.

106

While I Speak to Thee.

Tune—"I Hear Thy Welcome Voice."
  B. J. 55. S. M. 1., 276. Key,
  E. Flat.

1. Before Thy face, dear Lord,
  Myself I want to see;
And while I every question sing
  I want to answer Thee.

CHORUS.

While I speak to Thee,
    Lord, Thy goodness show;
Am I what I ought to be?
    O Saviour, let me know.

2. Am I what once I was?
    Have I that ground maintained
Wherein I walked in power with Thee,
    And Thou my soul sustained?

3. Do I possess a heart
    In thought and action clean?
From Monday morn till Sunday eve
    Has my salvation been?

4. Have I the zeal I had?
    When Thou didst me ordain
To preach Thy word and seek Thy lost,
    Or do I feel it pain?

5. Have I a truthful heart—
    A conscience quick to feel,
The baseness of a false excuse,
    The touch of what's unreal?

6. Do I my comrade slight,
    Or envy him his place?
Do I exaggerate his faults,
    Or speak behind his face?

7. Am I the one to go
    Where all is big and bright?
And have I lost the zeal I knew
    To share the hardest fight?

107

Nearer, My God, to Thee.

1. Nearer, my God, to Thee,
    Nearer to Thee,
E'en though it be a cross
    That raiseth me:
Still all my song shall be,
Nearer, my God, to Thee,
    Nearer to Thee!

2. Though like a wanderer,
    The sun gone down,
Darkness be over me,
    My rest a stone,
Yet in my dreams I'll be
Nearer, my God, to Thee,
    Nearer to Thee!

3. There let the way appear,
    Steps unto Heaven;
All that Thou sendest me,
    In mercy given:
Angels to beckon me
Nearer, my God, to Thee,
    Nearer to Thee!

4. Then, with my waking thoughts
    Bright with Thy praise,
Out of my stony griefs
    Bethel I'll raise:
So by my woes to be
Nearer, my God, to Thee,
    Nearer to Thee!

5. Or if, on joyful wing
    Cleaving the sky,
Sun, moon and stars forgot,
    Upward I fly,
Still all my song shall be,
Nearer, my God, to Thee,
    Nearer to Thee.

108

Jesus, Lover of My Soul.

Tune—"Jesus, Lover of My Soul."
    B. J. 181. S. M. II., 73. 7s.

1. Jesus, lover of my soul,
    Let me to Thy bosom fly,
While the nearer waters roll,
    While the tempest still is high.
Hide me, oh, my Saviour, hide,
    Till the storm of life is past,
Safe into the haven guide,
    Oh, receive my soul at last!

2. Other refuge have I none,
    Hangs my helpless soul on Thee:
Leave, ah, leave me not alone,
    Still support and comfort me.
All my trust on Thee is stayed,
    All my help from Thee I bring;
Cover my defenceless head
    With the shadow of Thy wing.

3. Plenteous grace with Thee is found,
    Blood to cleanse from every sin:
Let the healing streams abound,
    Make and keep me pure within.
Thou of life the fountain art;
    Freely let me take of Thee;
Spring Thou up within my heart,
    Rise to all eternity.

109

Come, oh, Come with Me.

1. Come, oh, come with me, where
    love is beaming,
Come, oh, come with me, where light
    is streaming.
Light and love divine, in Christ re-
    vealing
    God Himself to you and me.

CHORUS.

Hallelujah! hallelujah! I love Thee,
    my Saviour;
Hallelujah! hallelujah! I trust but in
    Thee.

2. Come with all your sins, although a
    mountain,
Come unto the Cross from whence a
    fountain
Flows divinely clear, to heal the na-
    tions,
    Come and wash and make you clean.

3. None can be too vile for love so
    beaming,
None can be too dark for light so
    streaming,
Christ will make you whole, thro' faith
    revealing
    Full salvation unto you.

4. Come and let us kneel, where Jesus
    meets us,
Let us ever stay where Christ receives
    us,
Safe within the fold no harm can
    reach us;
    Hasten, hasten to the fold.

110

No Night There.

BY COLONEL LAWLEY.

1. No night there but an endless day,
In that beautiful land far away, far
    away;
Our flower is blooming on hills of
    gold,
There is no night there, but joy un-
    told.

CHORUS.

No night there, no night there,
God is the light, there is no night
    there.

2. Why are ye troubled while here be-
    low,
When to that beautiful land we soon
    shall go?
Our precious Saviour His word has
    given,
Who bear His cross, shall share His
    Heaven.

3. No night there, no gath'ring gloom,
In the Father's bright hall is the chil-
    dren's room:
No care can oppress them, no storm
    affright,
No parting can sever, there'll be no
    night.

4. No night there by the crystal sea,
Nor sorrow nor death any more can
    be;
Oh, who would recall to a world like
    this,
The lambs that are folded on the hills
    of bliss?

111

It's Grand to be a Soldier.

Tune—"Duffy, the Swell."

1. It's grand to be a soldier, a warrior
    for our King:
It's grand to know that a crown we'll
    wear if we are but true to Him.
It's grand to have His presence felt,
    it's grand to know no fear:
It's grand to get away from self, it's
    grand to know He's here.

CHORUS.

Oh, this peace hasn't ceased since the
    world was first created!
And this love from above it makes us
    all related.
In His sight comes the light that seems
    to overfill us.
It's truly grand to take a stand for one
    so grand as He.

2. How grand of Him to suffer pain!
    How grand of Him to die!
How grand that in our hearts He
    reigns, His loving Spirit nigh!
How grand when clouds are darkest
    that we to Him can go!
He's the grandest of the greatest, it's
    grand to love Him so.

3. How grand of Him to warn us!
   In St. John it's written there.
I'll surely come amongst you, so work-
   ers be prepared.
In my Father's house are mansions
   for the faithful, brave and
   true;"
It's grand to know you're ready, it's
   grander with Him to go.

112

I Know of a Saviour from Sin.

WORDS BY COLONEL LAWLEY.

B. J. No. 171.

1. Some people I know don't live holy,
   They battle with unconquered sin,
Not daring to consecrate fully,
   Or they full salvation would win.
With malice they have constant
   trouble,
   From fearing they long to be free:
With most things about them they
   grumble,
   Praise God, this is not so with me!

CHORUS.

I know of a Saviour from sin,
I know of a Saviour from sin;
   Our almighty Jesus is able
   To keep even me without sin.

2. Some people are useless to Jesus,
   The reason is easy to find;
They're fighters when everything
   pleases,
   At other times hang on behind.
There are thousands I know join the
   doubters,
   While others backslide, I can see,
And some run away with the shouters,
   Praise God, this is not so with me!

3. Some people enjoy full salvation,
   Their peace like a river does flow,
With them there is no condemnation,
   The blood keeps them whiter than
   snow.
Well saved, praise the Lord, hallelu-
   jah!
Triumphant through Christ on the
   tree,
They bask in the sunshine of Beulah,
Praise God, this is just so with me!

113

I will Follow Thee, my Saviour.

B. J. 1. S. M., II., 67.

1. Jesus, I my cross have taken,
   All to leave and follow Thee;
Naked, poor, despised, forsaken,
   Thou from hence my all shalt be.
Perish every fond ambition,
   All I've sought, or hoped, or known!
Yet how rich is my condition!
   God and Heaven are still my own.

CHORUS.

I will follow Thee, my Saviour;
   Thou didst shed Thy blood for me:
And though all men should forsake
   Thee,
   By Thy grace I'll follow Thee.

2. Let the world despise and leave me,
   They have left my Saviour too;
Human hearts and looks deceive me;
   Thou art not like them, untrue;
And whilst Thou shalt smile upon me,
   God of wisdom, love and might,
Foes may hate and friends may shun
   me,
   Show Thy face and all is bright.

3. Men may trouble and distress me.
   'Twill but drive me to Thy breast:
Life with trials hard may press me.
   Heaven will bring me sweeter rest.
Oh, 'tis not in grief to harm me.
   While Thy love is left to me!
Oh, 'twere not in joy to charm me,
   Were that joy unmixed with Thee!

114

Calvary's Crimson River.

Tune—"Scatter Seeds of Kindness."

1. There is a crimson river
   Rising on Mount Calvary,
With its waters flowing ever
   Toward the mighty crimson sea;
For the healing of the nations
   Was this fountain opened wide,
That sin and all uncleanness
   Might be swept beneath its tide.

CHORUS.

Oh, Calvary's crimson river!
Oh, Calvary's crimson river!
Oh, Calvary's crimson river!
   Flows to wash thy sins away.

2. The Author of this river
   Was the Man of Galilee;
To become the world's life-giver
   Gave His life upon the tree.
He left His home in Heaven
   And His glory laid aside;
With a spear His side was riven
   Just to start this crimson tide.

3. O blessed crimson river,
   Of thy virtue all shall know!
It is written whosoever
   Will, may to thy waters go.
Though their sins may be as scarlet,
   Like as wool they soon will show.
If they're redder still like crimson,
   Thou canst wash them white as
       snow.

115

I'll Fight for Thee All the Way,

1. My Lord, I know that Thou want-
      est all
   Whom Thy precious blood has
      bought,
To leave their all and to take their
      place,
   Wherever Thy war is fought,
So I will obey Thee, and in Thy
      strength,
   I'll go to the front to-day,
And, true to Thy colors and cross
      till death,
   I'll fight for Thee all the way!

CHORUS.

I'll fight for Thee all the way, Lord!
   I'll fight for Thee all the way;
      Close beside me,
      Thou shalt guide me,
   And keep me through the fray;
And I shall be more than conq'ror,
   In darkness or in light,
      As on Thee relying,
      Thy foes all defying,
'll fight till the end of the fight.

2. I know the war will be fierce and
      hard,
   With a foe so bold and strong,
But well I know that Thy mighty
      pow'r
   Is great as my fight is long;
And Thou canst depend upon me,
      my Lord,

In ranks of Thy hosts to stay,
As Calvary's Cross every day I see,
   I'll fight for Thee all the way!

3. Myself and all that I have I give,
   As I've never done before,
Come health or sickness, come weal
      or woe,
   I'll die in Thy glorious war;
And if in my heart is left aught of
      self,
   Now purge me with fire, I pray,
Then, fearing no foe, I will take Thy
      sword
   And—fight for Thee all the way!

116

The Ballroom Experience Song.

WORDS BY BRIGADIER ADDIE.

Tune—"While the Dance Went On."

1. Across the floor of the ballroom,
   Amid the gay and the bright,
A crowd of dancers were waltzing,
   Seeming with joy and delight;
Madly the din of the music,
   Urging and driving them on,
Let come what may, nothing care they,
   While the dance went on.
Yet there was one in that ballroom—
   One who had fallen from grace,
Who could not join in the laughter,
   For he was out of place;
Still he kept playing the music,
   Trying his conscience to calm,
But 'twas in vain, worse grew the pain,
   While the dance went on.

CHORUS.

While the music was playing
   In the grand ballroom,
And dancers were dancing
   Heedless to their doom,
Instant, out of season
   One man, all alone,
Led a soul to Jesus
   While the dance went on.

2. A man of God who was passing,
   Just had returned to the town,
Where years ago he had labored,
   Seeking lost jewels for His crown;
Stopping to listen a moment,
   Feeling constrained to step in.
He climbed the stair, breathing a
      prayer,

While the dance went on.
Eager to strike for his Master,
He looked round on the scene,
Recognized one of the fiddlers,
Who once a Christian had been.
Had he forsaken his Saviour?
There it was only too plain;
Angels were sad, devils were glad,
While the dance went on.

3. Dancing had ceased for a moment,
God's hero seized on the chance,
Up to the backslidden fiddler
Fearlessly he did advance.
Handing him a piece of silver,
"Please will you play me a tune?"
"Yes, sir," said he; "What shall it
be?"
While the dance went on.
" 'The Bleeding Lamb' is its title,
Play it as in days gone by."
Down dropped the guilty backslider,
Trembling, for mercy did cry;
There on the floor of that ballroom
The Bleeding Lamb made him whole;
Some ran away, some stayed to pray,
While the dance went on.

117

Over Me.

Tune—"Sweet Marie."

WORDS BY MAJOR PEBBLES.

1. There's a sea for weary souls,
Crimson sea,
And its cleansing billows roll
Over me.
To this sea your sorrows bring,
And its waves will heal the sting,
It is flowing while I sing,
Over me.
Oh, what heavenly raptures steal
Over me,
Just when the waves I feel
Over me.
All my sins and sorrows go,
And my heart is white as snow,
While the cleansing billows flow
Over me.

CHORUS.

Over me, over me,
Over me, over me,
Let the mighty billows roll
Over me.

Let me bathe my weary soul,
Satisfy and make it whole,
While the cleansing billows roll
Over me.

2. There's an ocean full of love,
Love to me;
Love to God in Heaven above,
Love to me.
I, a rebel, full of guile,
And my heart was black and vile,
And He loved me all the while,
Even me.
Like an ocean wide and deep,
Love to me;
For sinners He did weep,
Even me.
By His grace He made me whole,
And His love now fills my soul;
Like a wave I feel it roll
Over me.

3. Grace is flowing like a river,
Grace for me;
Grace to bear me up for ever,
Grace for me.
Like a river it doth flow,
Free to all men here below;
That's enough for me, I know,
Even me.
It is flowing every day,
Grace for me.
Why should I from Him stray?
Grace for me.
By His grace He keeps me whole,
Keeps the victory in my soul,
Like a wave I feel it roll
Over me.

118

My Sins Rose as High as a Mountain.

Tune—"Wonderful Words of Life."
G Flat.

1. I've heard of a Saviour whose love
was so strong,
He loved a poor sinner like me;
He turned His back on a glorified
throng,
To save a poor sinner like me.
The angels they sang Him from
Glory,
I'm glad that they told me the story,
He came from on high to suffer and
die,
To save a poor sinner like me.

My sins rose as high as a mountain,
They all disappeared in the Fountain,
He put my name down for a palace
    and crown,
    Bless His dear name, I am free!

2 This wonderful Saviour took such
    a low place,
    To save a poor sinner like me:
His heart overflowing with wondrous
    grace,
    To save a poor sinner like me.
Was born in a stable and manger,
In His own world was a stranger,
With all things did part to win my
    hard heart,
    And save a poor sinner like me.

3 This Jesus had nowhere to lay His
    head,
    To save a poor sinner like me:
He was a Lamb to the slaughter led,
    To save a poor sinner like me.
'Midst darkness my Saviour is dying,
" 'Tis finished!" I hear Jesus crying:
My soul may go free, He died on the
    tree,
    To save a poor sinner like me.

119
Sinner, See Yon Light.

Tune—"Sinner, See Yon Light." B.
    J. 48.

Sinner, see yon light
Shining clear and bright
    From the Cross on Calvary;
Where the Saviour died,
And from His side
    Came the Blood that sets us free.

CHORUS.

Come away, come away,
Come away, come away,
    To the Cross for refuge flee:
See, the Saviour stands
With His bleeding hands,
    Thy ransom He paid on the tree.

2. In the gloomy shade
When He knelt and prayed,
    Oh, what painful agony!
When His brow was wet
With the bloody sweat
    In the Garden of Gethsemane.

3. See, the Saviour stands
With His wounded hands,
    And He calls aloud to thee,
"I for thee life gave,
Thy soul to save:
    Then thy heart now give to Me."

4 Come away to Him
And confess your sin;
    Come to Him who died for thee.
To His feet draw near
With a heart sincere,
    And from sin He'll set thee free.

120
Why wilt Thou Die?

Tune—"Why Wilt Thou Die?" B. J.
    171. S. M. II., 50.

Sinner, for thee,
A pardon so free,
Though dark thy career may have
    been,
    The burden shall roll
    From thy guilty soul
When the light of His face thou hast
    seen.

CHORUS.

Oh, why wilt thou die?
Why wilt thou die?
Sinner, sinner, why?

2. Tired of thy sin,
    And sorrow within,
Thy soul longs to find its true joy—
    The joy that thy King
    In mercy doth bring
Thy sorrow and sin to destroy.

3. Death is at hand
    Thy life to demand,
Make haste, now, the Saviour to find;
    No longer delay,
    You're passing away,
And Satan your soul wants to bind.

4. Awful despair
    Thy bosom will tear
When Heaven for thee has no room—
    For ever shut out,
    In darkness and doubt,
Then Hell everlasting thy doom.

121

Will You be Saved To-night?

BY MAJOR J. C. LUDGATE.

Tune — "Where is My Wandering
Boy To-night?"

1. Oh, will you not yield to God to-
night?
Too long you have spurned His
grace;
Your life has been spent in sin and
wrong,
But there is abundant grace.

CHORUS.

Oh, will you be saved to-night?
Oh, will you be saved to-night?
Salvation free is now offered thee;
Oh, will you be saved to-night?

2. Go to the Lord for peace to-night;
Go seek Him, He loves you still;
Your friend He will be, He waits for
thee,
Submit to His holy will.

3. Oh, the sweet peace and holy joy
The Lord on thy soul will pour,
When all your heart to Him you
bring,
And from Him you wander no more.

122

Poor Sinner to Jesus Come Home.

Tune—"Sinner, Come Home." B. J.
117. S. M. II., 6.

1. Sinner, poor sinner, to Jesus come
home,
He long has been calling for thee;
No longer delay, but come while you
may,
The saved and the happy to be.
Your days swiftly fly, and soon you
must die,
And then the dread judgment will
come;
In vain then to call on the mountains
to fall,
And hide you from Him on the
Throne.

CHORUS.

Come home, come home, come home,
Poor sinner, to Jesus come home.

2. Sinner, poor sinner, then wilt thou
not turn
And accept a salvation so free?
There's nought to be done, but only to
come;
Thy Saviour is waiting for thee.
Oh, soon will the day of His grace
pass away,
Then judgment will visit for sin:
But now there is room, the vilest may
come,
"Compel them," He says, "to come
in."

123

He'll Take You to His Fold Again.

Tune—"Kathleen."

1. He'll take you to His fold again,
Poor sinner, though you far have
strayed,
No longer in your sins remain,
For One is strong enough to save.
Thy Saviour, who has loved thee so,
And left His all for thee to die,
His Blood will wash you white as
snow,
If to His loving arms you'll fly.

CHORUS.

He'll take you to His fold again,
And wash your heart from every
stain,
And though you may be grieving sore,
He'll take you to His fold again.

2. Before you let your love grow cold,
Your heart was always fond and
true,
You sought to bring the lost to Him,
Who now is yearning over you.
He weeps to see you leave the path,
Wherein you once did run so well.
A loving welcome now He'll give,
If you will come with Him to dwell.

3. His Spirit gently strives to win
An entrance to your stricken heart,
Oh, stay no longer in your sin,
Or soon His striving may depart.
Soon death will call thee and they'll
lay
Thy cold, cold form beneath the sod:
Then, sinner, haste, oh, haste away,
And get thy soul at peace with God.

124

Always the Same is Jesus.

Tune—"Always the Same is Jesus."

1. Always the same is Jesus,
   In Him no change I find,
   He to my soul is precious,
   True, loving, good and kind.
   Though sorrows may o'ertake me,
   And friends to help be few,
   Though all the world forsake me,
   Jesus will always be true.

CHORUS.

I have a Friend who is always the
   same,
Always the same, bless His dear name:
I have a Friend who is always the
   same,
   Never I've known Him to change.

2. Always the same is Jesus,
   Never His love has failed:
   Always the same—so gracious,
   When by the foe assailed;
   Always the same, no matter
   How dark the way may seem:
   Always my path seems brighter
   When it is lit up by Him.

3. Always the same is Jesus; •
   Why should I doubt or fear?
   His grace to me is boundless,
   His love my spirit cheers.
   How can I be downhearted
   While I have such a Friend?
   Knowing for Heaven I've started,
   He'll guide me safe to the end.

125

Friendship with Jesus.

BY MAJOR J. C. LUDGATE.

Tune — "Massa's in the Cold, Damp
   Ground."

1. A friend of Jesus, oh, what bliss,
   That one so vile as I
   Should ever have a Friend like this
   To lead me to the sky.

CHORUS.

Friendship with Jesus, fellowship
   divine:
   Oh, what blessed, sweet communion—
Jesus is a Friend of mine.

2. A Friend when other friendships
      cease,
   A Friend when others fail;
   A Friend who gives me joy and peace,
   A Friend who will prevail.

3. A Friend to lead me in the dark,
   A Friend who knows the way;
   A Friend to steer my weak, frail bark,
   A Friend my debts to pay.

4. A Friend when sickness lays me
      low:
   A Friend when death draws near;
   A Friend as through the vale I go,
   A Friend to help and cheer.

5. A Friend when life's short race is
      o'er,
   A Friend when earth is past;
   A Friend to meet on Heaven's shore,
   A Friend when home at last.

126

I'm Sure I'm Saved.

1. I've said adieu to the devil's crew
   And joined a happier lot;
   Instead of going down to Hell
   Salvation I have got.
   My heart, I know, is white as snow,
   Christ does with me abide;
   I care not what the world may say,
   I'm on the winning side.

CHORUS.

I know, I'm sure, my heart is white
      as snow,
   And if I die to Heaven I shall go:
From sin and shame my soul has been
      set free.
   And oh, I'm glad to tell you, salva-
tion is for thee!

2. For God I fight with all my might,
   Wherever I may go;
   I praise the Lord I'm not ashamed
   To let the people know
   That I belong to the happy throng
   Who've had their sins forgiven;
   I'll fight for God until I die,
   And then I'll go to Heaven.

3. Now every soul can be made whole,
   For Jesus wants to save,
   That you might be redeemed from sin

His own life's Blood He gave;
And if to-day you'll leave the way
That leads to endless woe,
He'll wash you in His precious Blood,
And make you white as snow.

127

The Gospel Ship.

Tune—"The Ship that Never Re-
turned."

1. The Gospel ship at anchor is lying,
She is booked to sail to-day;
To fill her state-rooms her agents are
trying,
They are giving the tickets away.
Her steam is up, her flag is flying,
There's a crowd but room for more:
Come and pass the Doctor—He'll take
you if you're dying—
She is bound for Canaan's shore.

CHORUS.

Will she ever return? No, she'll never
return,
For 'tis better on before;
It's a land that flows with milk and
honey,
She is bound for Canaan's shore.

2. On board she has first-class accom-
modation,
No dividing ropes you'll find;
Her passengers, whatever their sta-
tion,
Are all bound by cords divine.
Her crew is saved and sanctified,
King Jesus—her Captain's name—
'Twas to navigate this ship He died,
And down from Glory came.

3. Her starting place is the famed Red
River,
That flows from the Captain's side;
She sails on time independent of
weather,
And she waits not for the tide.
The winds may blow and the storm-
clouds gather,
They obey the Captain's will;
His power is the same to-day and
forever—
It was Christ said: "Peace, be still!"

128

Afar From God.

Tune—"Marguerite."

1. Afar from God in weariness and
sin,
Thy soul has wandered many years;
And drinking deep of pleasure's cup,
Has quaffed its bitter tears,
Weary one.
The day is short'ning, ere its sun has
set,
To Jesus turn, there's mercy still;
He loves and longs, with deep desire,
Thy soul to fill,
Weary one.

2. Away from childhood's home and
innocence,
In sin's delusive toils ensnared;
Forgetting mother's prayers and tears,
Nor thought that Jesus cared,
Weary one.
Yet mercy's gates were always open
wide;
True joy and peace were ever there,
And Jesus now is waiting here
To answer prayer.
Weary one.

3. He will not chide thee for the sinful
past,
Nor turn aside thy tempted soul;
With love as boundless as 'tis free,
He will forgive the whole.
Weary one.
Nor back to bondage shall thy foot-
steps slide,
Thy life no more be spoiled by sin;
His blood will keep thee every hour
All pure within.
Weary one.

129

Take Back Thy Heart to the Saviour.

Tune — "Take Back the Heart that
Thou Gavest."

1. Take back thy heart to the Saviour,
Think of His anguish for thee;
Take back thy heart to the Saviour,
Now He is calling for thee;
Thou hast rejected His mercy,
Oft spurned His pardon so free;
Still He beholds you in pity,
Now He is calling for thee.

CHORUS.

Take back thy heart to the Saviour,
  Think of His anguish for thee;
Take back thy heart to the Saviour,
  Now He is calling for thee.

2. Once in His footsteps you traveled,
  Followed while He chose the way,
Sorrow was turned into gladness,
  Darkness had turned into day;
But in the hour of temptation,
  From His dear arms you did flee;
Hasten and seek His forgiveness,
  Now He is calling for thee.

3. Death and destruction are coming,
  Coming to drag you away;
Hope will forever be gone then,
  Rush to His arms while you may;
He will forgive you and bid you
  From your backslidings be free;
Take back thy heart to the Saviour,
  Now He is calling for thee.

130
I'm Trusting in My Saviour.

Tune—"The Girl I Left Behind."

1. I am trusting in my Saviour,
Trusting when my faith is small,
He gives to me His joy without alloy;
Though at times the devil tempts me,
From this narrow road to roam,
'Tis then my Saviour Satan's powers
    destroy.
Oh, 'tis good to live for Jesus,
Yes, 'tis grand to do His will,
For then He smiles upon me,
And with joy my heart does fill;
I will ever trust His promise,
Ever be His soldier true,
And then I will be with Him
In Heaven to dwell.

CHORUS.

Come, sinner, just now,
  At His feet lowly bow,
He's waiting to set you free;
He suffered and died, was crucified,
  On Calvary's cruel tree.

2. I was wandering from the Saviour,
Knowing naught of His dear love,
Because I would not seek His blessed
    face;

Yet His Spirit ne'er forsook me,
But it showed me I was wrong,
And praise the Lord, I came and found
  His grace;
And He gives to me His pardon,
And salvation full and free,
And now His precious blood has saved
And pardoned even me.
Now, poor sinner, He is waiting,
With His love to welcome you,
And then He'll save your soul
And set you free.

131
I'll Stay in the Army.
Tune—"The Ship I Love."

1. Some say the Army should not
    march
  The streets or beat their drum;
But what would all our soldiers do
  To make the people come?
They hear the church bells ringing
    loud,
  From steeples short and tall,
Although they know the meaning well,
  They do not heed the call.

CHORUS.

I'll stay in the Army,
  Walk in the light;
Now nothing can harm me,
  While battling for right;
For Jesus, my Captain, now
  Tells me to never fear,
I'll follow wherever He leads me,
  For He is always near.

2. There has been many a drunkard,
Many a gambler, too,
Brought from the haunts of sin and
    vice
  To soldiers brave and true;
And many a home is happy now,
  And glad that the Army's here,
And now we're here to tell you
  Of a Saviour's love so dear.

132
I Love Him Best of All.
BY MAJOR PEBBLES.
Tune—"I Love You in Spite of All."

1. Many a friend I've known; hearts
    that were brave and true;
Sharing each grief and sorrow, as
    earthly friends can do;

Smiling when all is bright, weeping
when clouds hang low,
True friends in the time of affliction,
true in the hour of woe.
But I have a Friend who tasted death
for all,
He loved me when a stranger—I love
Him best of all.

CHORUS.

I love Him best of all, He is my dearest Friend;
By His own blood He saved me. He'll
keep me to the end.
With His own hand to guide me I care
not what befall,
He will not leave nor forsake me—I
love Him best of all.

2. Moments of joy I've known, when
all this world seemed bright,
All nature smiled with gladness, teem-
ing with pure delight;
Song-birds were on the wing, chant-
ing their merry lay,
And earth, like Eden, was blooming
with the sweet flowers of May;
But the charms of earth, as leaves in
Autumn, fall,
When I behold His beauty I love Him
best of all.

3. Soon shall I say farewell, bid you a
long good night,
Finish my earthly warfare, pass to the
realms of light;
There I shall see that throng—oh,
what a sight 'twill be!
And hear them shouting "Hosanna!"
through all eternity.
There I shall see Jesus, down before
Him fall,
And sing with heavenly rapture, "I
love Him best of all!"

133
The Holy City.

Tune—"Banks of the Wabash."

1. There's a city where no sorrow ever
enters,
And where death and partings
nevermore are known;
But where peace and joy and gladness
reign forever,

And where God our Father sits upon
the Throne,
The angels hover round to do His
bidding,
And nothing that they do delight
them more,
Than to sing and shout a hallelujah
welcome
To the blood-washed as they near
the golden shore.

CHORUS.

The lights are shining bright along the
river,
And the angels sing a welcome from
the shore;
We shall dwell among the saints in
yonder city,
On the banks of life's river evermore.

2. When the warfare and the strife on
earth are ended,
And the soldiers muster for the
grand review;
When the King shall hand rewards out
to the faithful,
We'll be glad we stood and fought
the battle through.
We shall walk through the streets of
the city,
With patriarchs and prophets we
shall meet,
And when we see the King in all His
beauty,
We will cast our crowns together at
His feet.

3. In that city on the banks of life's
pure river,
There are mansions all prepared for
you and me:
And it hath not entered man's heart
to imagine,
All the sights and sounds that we
shall hear and see.
When we view our Saviour's form in
that picture,
And marks of all His suffering we
can trace,
We will praise Him ever through
eternal ages,
When we meet Him up in Heaven
face to face.

134

Tell Them Jesus Loves Them.

Tune—"The Sweetest Story Ever Told."

1 Round the world the Army chariot
    now rolls;
For Jesus we are saving precious souls,
And telling all abroad that Jesus died
On the cross for all was crucified.
Tell it o'er again that story old,
The dearest, sweetest story ever told;
Tell it to the outcast sunken low,
Tell it to the lost where'er you go.

CHORUS.

Tell them Jesus loves them,
    And His love is purer far than gold;
Tell them Jesus loves them,
    For 'tis the sweetest story ever told.
        (Repeat.)

2. Broken-hearted, many wander every
    day,
Enchained and led by Satan all the
    way,
But these are they whom Jesus died
    to save;
O comrades, let the crimson banner
    wave!
Tell it o'er again that story old,
The dearest, sweetest story ever told;
Tell the weary ones by sin oppressed,
That Jesus waits to give them peace
    and rest.

SECOND CHORUS.

Tell them Jesus loves them,
And that His love for them will ne'er
    grow cold;
Tell them Jesus loves them,
For 'tis the sweetest story ever told.

135

That is Love.

Tune—"That is Love."

1. Have you a friend that is always
    nigh?
Have you a friend that for you would
    die?
Have you a friend his life would give,
Lay down his life that you might live?
For your iniquities and your sins be
    bruised,

Bear all the stripes that from sin you
    might be excused,
Jesus, the Saviour, came down from
    Heaven above,
For sinners was slain. Oh, that is
    love!

CHORUS.

All the way to Calvary He went for
    me,
Bore my sin and guilt and shame upon
    the tree;
Like a lamb to slaughter led His
    life He gave,
Hear Him say, "I die that they might
    live!"
That is love! That is love!

2. Bruised and bleeding in sin we lay,
Hoping not for a brighter day.
Lost to Heaven and lost to God,
Naught for us but the chastening rod;
Death was the sentence and Hell be-
    yond the grave,
No eye to pity, no arm was there to
    save;
But Jesus tasted death that we might
    live,
He tasted death for all. Oh, that is
    love!

3. Would you the love of the Saviour
    know,
With Him to Heaven triumphant go,
With Him upon a throne sit down,
From Him receive a starry crown;
Hear from His lips, "Well done, my
    child, well done,"
Shine forth forever in Heaven like as
    the sun;
Show Him your love by seeking the lost
    to save,
And finding His lambs. Oh, that is
    love!

136

He Never Cares to Wander.

BY STAFF-CAPTAIN J. C. LUDGATE.

Tune—"He Never Cares to Wander
    from His Own Fireside."

1. Many men of many habits,
    Some prefer to cross the tide.
Roaming all this wide world over
    All in vain their sins to hide.

But there's one of whom I'll tell you,
He's the pattern man for me;
In our Army you will find him
O'er this land from sea to sea.

CHORUS.

He never cares to wander from his
    Saviour's side.
    He never cares to wander or to
    roam;
With his comrades, you can see, he's
    as happy as can be,
    For there's no place like home, sweet
    home.

2. 'Twas the Army's dress and music
That first caught his eye and ear;
Now the hallelujah war-paint
    He is wearing without fear,
With his cap and badge and S's.
And his guernsey bright and red.
He's a sign-post, warning sinners
    Who the downward road would
    tread.

3. Sinner, you who sit and listen
To the song we sing to-night.
Will you give your heart to Jesus—
Leave the wrong and do the right?
If you do He'll make you happy
And your sins He'll wash away.
Then with all your happy comrades
Altogether you can say—

137
I Am Neither Rich Nor Lucky.

BY STAFF-CAPTAIN J. C. LUDGATE.

Tune — "She Was Bred in Old Kentucky."

1. Once a letter came one day from a
    country far away
    To a mother from her wandering.
    wayward boy.
He had caused her many tears. she
    had wished and hoped for years
    That he would become to her a cheer
    and joy.
Tremblingly she broke the seal, dreading what it might reveal.
Expecting news of death or sickness
    there.
But as line by line she read. kneeling
    there beside her bed,
This is what the wanderer's letter to
    her said:

CHORUS.

I am neither rich nor lucky, but I
    know I'm saved to-day;
My sins are all forgiven, I am bound
    for endless day;
When I cried, "Lord Jesus, save me."
Joy and peace and light He gave me,
And He'll do the very same for you.

2. "Mother, dear," the note began, "I
    am now a different man;
    For I've left the path of sin and
    shame and wrong;
I have given God my heart. and for
    Heaven made a start,
    And I daily pray the Lord to make
    me strong.
'Twas an Army open-air standing in
    the market square
Made me stop and listen to the words
    of life;
There I heard how Jesus died. on the
    Cross was crucified,
And I promised God I'd leave my sinful life.

3. "Now, dear mother, I shall pray
    we may meet again some day,
    And I hope to bless and cheer your
    waning years;
I am sorry for the past, when in sin I
    rushed so fast,
    And my folly made you shed those
    bitter tears.
I shall daily pray for you, that the
    Lord will keep us true.
    And if on earth we never meet
    again.
On that happy golden shore may we
    meet to part no more,
    And with Jesus and our loved ones
    we shall reign.

138
Hornets.

BY BRIGADIER ADDIE.

*And I sent the hornet before you
which drove them out from before
you, even the two kings of the Amorites. but not with thy sword, nor
with thy bow.*—Joshua 24: 12.

Tune—"Let the Dear Master Come
    In."

1. When the Canaanites hardened
    their hearts against God,
    And grieved Him because of their
    sin,

He sent along hornets to bring them
  to time,
  And help His own people to win.
The hornets persuaded them that it was
  best
  To move quick and not to be slow;
They did not compel them to go
  'gainst their will,
  They just made them willing to go.

CHORUS.

The last two lines of each verse.

2 If a nest of live hornets was
  brought to this room
  And the creatures allowed to go
  free.
You would not need urging to make
  yourself scarce,
  You'd want to get out, don't you
  see?
They would not lay hold and by dint
  of their strength
  Throw you out of the window—no,
  no!
They would not compel you to go
  'gainst your will,
They'd just make you willing to go.

3. When Jonah was sent to start Nin-
  eveh corps
  The outlook was not very bright;
He never had done such a hard thing
  before,
  So he flunked and ran off from the
  fight.
He was caught and imprisoned inside
  a great fish;
  The story I'm sure you all know.
God did not compel him to go 'gainst
  his will,
  He just made him willing to go.

4 When Balaam was sent with the
  princes of Moab
  He wanted things run his own way;
But his ass, ever faithful, spake at
  the right time,
  Made him willing God's voice to
  obey.
God can use any man since He used
  Balaam's ass,
  For He is almighty you know;
You need not compel folks to go
  'gainst their will,
  You just make them willing to go.

139

Just as the Sun Went Down.

BY BRIGADIER J. C. ADDIE.

Tune—"Just as the Sun Went Down."

1. After the din of the battle's roar,
  Just at the close of day;
Wounded and bleeding upon the field,
  Jesus, our Saviour, lay.
They pierced His side, nailed His
  hands, His feet,
  With thorns they made a crown;
"Father, forgive them," He cried, and
  died
  Just as the sun went down.

CHORUS.

He thought of sinners until the end
  As on the cross He lay;
Said to the thief that was by His
  side,
  "With Me thou'lt be to-day."
He came to seek and to save the lost;
  This was His joy and crown.
"Father, forgive them!" He cried, and
  died
  Just as the sun went down.

2. While He was hanging upon the
  cross,
  Giving His life away,
They took His garments each one a
  part,
  Mocking, they hear Him pray.
Rended were rocks, while the earth
  did quake;
  Heaven on high did frown,
Darkness came over the land and skies
  Just as the sun went down.

3. He came to earth from His home
  above,
  Beautiful, bright and fair;
Thinking of sinners, He laid aside
  All of His glory there.
He bore the mocking and scorn of
  men,
  Toiling from town to town;
Man was redeemed upon Calvary
  Just as the sun went down.

140

The Army Hat.

BY BRIGADIER ADDIE.

Tune—"Where Did You Get That
Hat?"

1. As I go walking down the street,
   I note the people stare;
They look at me from top to toe, and
   think I'm not all there;
But still I march along, not caring
   much for that,
Until I hear the boys cry out: "Where
   did you get that hat?"

CHORUS.

"Where did you get that hat?" the
   boys cry after me;
I wear it just for Jesus wherever I
   may be.
Oh, won't you come and wear one
   just the same as that?
Then you'll be so happy wearing the
   Army hat.

2. I'm glad I am a soldier and fighting for the Lord;
And tho' we dress peculiar, it's ac-
   cording to His Word;
And tho' the people slight us, we
   know what we are at;
We know we have got salvation, that's
   why we wear the hat.

3. Now, sinner, come and listen, and
   at Christ's footstool bow;
Come, kneel down at the cross, and
   He will save you now;
And when you've got salvation, and on
   the platform sit,
You'll know why we are happy, wear-
   ing the Army hat.

141

Chicago Slums

Tune—"A Little Lost Child."

1. A true-hearted Captain in Chicago
   Slums,
Just like an angel, pure and white, she
   comes
Into a haunt where God alone can tell
All the sin and crime within that
   earthly hell.
"Out of here!" said one; "get out of
   here," I say!
"Please, sir," said she, kindly, "won't
   you let me pray?"

"Well, if you must pray, then just go
   over there—
In the corner find a subject for your
   prayer."

CHORUS.

Whiter than snow; yes, far whiter;
   His blood makes whiter than
   snow! (twice)
"And tho' they be red like crimson,"
   when we to the fountain go,
Whiter than snow, it cleanses, I know;
His blood washes whiter than snow.

2. A poor fallen girl down in the
   corner lay:
Round her the shadows of death are
   drawing nigh.
"Do you know Jesus?" said the Cap-
   tain low.
"Shall I sing and pray with you be-
   fore I go?"
"Yes, I once knew Jesus in my
   mother's home;
Now I am forsaken, dying all alone."
She raised her white hand, and said,
   "Oh, can it be
Jesus, will You save a poor lost girl
   like me?"

3. The night had not passed when,
   down in the slum,
Angels of light in fiery chariots come,
Followed the footsteps of the Captain
   there.
Down into the corner where she knelt
   in prayer;
There they found a soul redeemed
   through Jesus' blood,
Bore her from the slums to realms
   of joy above.
When Captain Johnson home to
   Heaven comes,
A poor girl will greet her from Chi-
   cago Slums.

142

The Wanderer's Return.

1. In a lone cottage not far down the
   way,
Live an old couple with hair silv'ry
   gray.
Mourning the loss of a prodigal son,
One as the light of their eyes, but
   now gone—

F

Gone on the broad road of sin and de-
    spair,
Wander'd away from a fond mother's
    care,
Gone with companions so thoughtless
    and gay,
Still do his parents unceasingly pray.

CHORUS.

"Heavenly Father, bless our prodigal
    boy!
Heavenly Father, Satan would destroy
    our darling!
Jesus, Jesus, Lamb for sinners slain,
Save our boy, save our boy,
Bring him safe home again.

2. "Father, we've heard that Salva-
    tionists true
Live in this dark world seeking lost
    souls for You,
Into the dark haunts of sin daily go
Wonderful love of a Saviour to show;
Holding out hope to those fast in sin's
    thralls:
Maybe our boy is in one of their
    halls.
Then, mighty Spirit, take hold of him
    there,
Bring him down low at Thy footstool
    in prayer."

3. Should that poor prodigal be here
    to-night
Who on the hopes of his parents
    brought blight,
If he will now at the cross own his
    guilt,
Jesus is here, and for such His blood
    spilt;
Blood that avails to remove every
    stain.
If he by faith will but claim it again,
And all the joybells of Heaven will
    ring.
While with thanksgiving his parents
    will sing.

SECOND CHORUS.

"Glory, glory, God lives to answer
    pray'r!
Glory, glory, this we will declare to
    all men!
Glory, glory, thro' God's redeeming
    scheme.
There's a sea flowing free,
Making the vilest clean!"

4. Hear, blessed Saviour, my cry unto
    Thee.
Blot out the past and from sin set me
    free;
Free from the past with its misery
    and shame,
Saviour. I dare to believe on Thy
    name.
Oh! hallelujah! I feel the blood flow!
Cleansing and making me whiter
    than snow.
Now to Thy glory I'll spend all my
    days:
With my dear parents this glorious
    theme raise.

143
The Old Corps that Brought Me to the Fold.
BY BRIGADIER ADDIE.

1. I've been thinking to-day of that
    corps far away,
Its memories are worth more than
    gold:
    Oh! the joy that I felt at the cross
    as I knelt
    In the old corps that brought me to
    the fold.

CHORUS.

The old corps that brought me to the
    fold,
The old corps that brought me to the
    fold;
    While upon earth I stay I will never
    cease to pray
For the old corps that brought me to
    the fold.

2. The wanderer may roam, but there's
    no place like home—
No dearer spot his eyes can behold:
I have seen many a corps, but there's
    none I love more
    Than the old corps that brought
    me to the fold.

3. The soldiers were true, though the
    hundreds were few,
    And there's many standing yet I am
    told:
    Some are officers to-day, and they
    first learned to pray
    In the old corps that brought me to
    the fold.

4. It has altered a bit, this I frankly
admit,
And some things are not as of old;
It may have faults and flaws, yet I love
it just because
It's the old corps that brought me to
the fold.

5. I admit what you say, that the corps
of to-day
Are better than the corps were of
old,
They're advanced in every way, yet my
heart oft does stray
To the old corps that brought me to
the fold.

6. May its flag ever fly till sweet by-
and-by,
May many in its ranks be enrolled,
And in the glory-land I will shake
them by the hand,
The old corps that brought me to the
fold.

144 In a Graveyard Lonely.

BY BRIGADIER ADDIE.

Tune—"Tell Me With Your Eyes."

1. In a graveyard lonely, many miles
away,
Lies your dear old mother, 'neath
the cold, cold clay.
Memories now returning of her tears
and sighs,
If you love your mother, meet her in
the skies.

CHORUS.

Listen to her pleading, "Wandering
boy, come home,"
Lovingly entreating, do no longer
roam,
Let thy manhood waken, Heavenward
lift thine eyes,
If you love your mother, meet her in
the skies.

2. Now the old home vacant has no
charm for you,
One dear form is absent—mother kind
and true;
Where she dwells forever pleasure
never dies—
If you love your mother, meet her in
the skies.

3. Sacred vows you've broken in your
wayward life,
Strongest pledges spoken, forgotten in
the strife;
Hope has almost left you, wilt thou not
be wise?
If you love your mother, meet her in
the skies.

145 One Cold Winter's Eve.

Tune—"Kathleen Mavourneen."

1. One cold Winter's eve, when the
snow was fast falling,
In a small humble cottage a poor
mother lay;
Although racked with pain she lay
there contented,
With Christ as her Friend and her
peace with Him made

CHORUS.

We shall all meet again on that
great Judgment Morning,
The books will be opened, the roll will
be called;
How sad it will be if forever we are
parted,
And shut out of Heaven for not loving
God!

2. That mother of yours has gone over
death's river;
You promised you'd meet her as you
knelt by her side;
As the death sweat rolled off her and
fell on the pillow;
Her memory yet speaketh, altho' she
is dead.

3. You remember the kiss and the last
word that she uttered;
The arms that embraced you are
mouldering away;
As you stood by her grave and tears
dropped on her coffin,
With a vow that you'd meet her you
walked slowly away.

4. My brother, my sister, get ready to
meet her,
The life that you now live is ebbing
away.
But the life that's to come lasts forever and ever—
We may meet ne'er to part on that
great Judgment Day.

146

It's Rolling In.

1. The sea of God's eternal love,
   Is rolling in, is rolling in;
   Its current's deep and strong and
       wide;
   It's rolling in, it's rolling in;
   Upon its waves new hope it brings,
   Of constant vict'ry over sin;
   This blessed work it now begins,
   It's rolling in, it's rolling in.

CHORUS.

It's rolling in, it's rolling in,
The sea of love is rolling in;
Lord, I believe; Lord, I receive,
The Spirit's love is rolling in.

With love for souls my life possess—
   It's rolling in, it's rolling in;
With fiery zeal now fill my breast—
   It's rolling in, it's rolling in;
And through me let Thy treasures
       pour,
That weary hearts that now are sore,
May feel Thy touch of love once
       more—
   It's rolling in, it's rolling in.

147

The Drunkard's Song.

1. I have something now to say to
       you,
   And you will admit before I am
       through
   That what I'm going to say is right
       and just,
   For no matter where you be
   There are mortals you will see,
   On whom you gaze in horror and dis-
       gust,
   Though the man on whom you frown
   May be poor and broken down,
   And pressed by cold misfortune to the
       wall,
   Just lend to him a hand,
   For you must understand,
   There is a God above who died for all.

CHORUS.

Then if you should ever meet a poor
       drunkard on the street,
   Pity him, but don't condemn, I pray,
For it was rum that brought him low,
And his cup is filled with woe;
   He may become a sober man some
       day.

2. Did you ever stop to think that
       before he took to drink,
   He may have been some mother's
       only boy?
   Once so happy, bright and free as he
       sat upon her knee;
   'Twas then to him a life without
       alloy.
   No doubt to him she said, as she
       brushed his curly head,
   "Some day, my boy, you'll rise to
       wealth and fame!"
   But alas! poor mother's gone, and her
       boy is broken down,
   Through rum and beer he's brought
       to open shame.

3. Then perhaps, his wife at home, as
       she waits for him to come,
   With broken heart her lot she does
       bewail,
   As she prays to God above, to look
       down on him in love,
   And save her man from going to the
       jail.
   Then the children in the cot, sharing
       mother's wretched lot,
   Perhaps through cold and hunger
       fell asleep,
   While their father drinking rum in
       some tavern in the town,
   His promise made to wife he could
       not keep.

148

God's Salvation Army

Tune—"The Sidewalks of New York."

1. God's Salvation Army, with music
       and with song,
   Is ever on the highways to reach the
       giddy throng,
   Though with means peculiar, God has
       blessed the work
   Over all the Union, right from 'Frisco
       to New York.

CHORUS.

Inside, outside, all around the town,
Our Army helps the helpless, lifts the
       fallen when they're down;
Homes have been made happy, Heaven
       has blessed our work
Over all the Union, right from 'Frisco
       to New York.

2. Down among the lost ones, our brave
    slum angels live,
To bless and save the lowest their lives
    they freely give;
Spreading joy and sunshine, Heaven
    has blessed our work
Over all the Union, right from 'Frisco
    to New York.

3. At the prison gateway brigades now
    take their stand,
Ever ready waiting to lend a helping
    hand;
Thousands have been rescued, Heaven
    has blessed our work
Over all the Union, right from 'Frisco
    to New York.

4. Seeking for the fallen out upon the
    street,
Our rescue homes have sisters who
    any night you'll meet,
Seeking — aye, and finding; Heaven
    has blessed our work,
Over all the Union, right from 'Frisco
    to New York.

5. Food and shelter depots, where hun-
    gry crowds are fed,
And homeless men in thousands are
    nightly given a bed;
We care for souls and bodies, Heaven
    has blessed our work
Over all the Union, right from 'Frisco
    to New York.

149

Down in Poverty Row.

Tune—"Down in Poverty Row."

1. Within a crowded tenement where
    poorest folks abound,
    There dwell two Army slumming
    girls, the best that can be found;
They live just like their neighbors, an
    important point, you know,
    When they all things become, to
    their God they win some,
    Down in Poverty Row.

CHORUS.

Down in Poverty Row you will find
    our girls,
    Dredging cesspools of sin for those
    precious pearls,
God's love differeth not to the high or
    low,

Rich jewels and rare often lie buried
    there,
    Down in Poverty Row.

2. They go about among the poor, re-
    lieving want and pain:
    With pail and scrubbing-brush and
    soap an entrance soon they gain;
They nurse the children and the sick,
    spread joy where'er they go,
    They tell of a cure that is certain
    and sure,
    Down in Poverty Row.

3. Slum angels by the folks they're
    called, a name not far astray:
    In ministering to needy souls they
    work both night and day;
They care for souls and bodies, like
    the Master did, you know,
    For the Bible does tell with the poor
    He did dwell,
    Down in Poverty Row.

150

Fallen by the Wayside.

BY MAJOR PEBBLES.

Tune—"Fallen by the Wayside."

1. On a cold and dreary pavement
    stood a woman poorly dressed,
Not a friend on earth was left her but
    the child upon her breast;
On her pale cheeks tears are falling,
    and her heart is broke with grief,
She is going to the river for relief.
'Tis nothing new, betrayed, deserted,
Cast on the world a withered flower,
    from which the fragrance all has
    gone;
Someone's darling has been sacrificed
    upon the shrine of lust,
She is only one among that wretched
    throng.

CHORUS.

See, the Saviour stands beside her,
Wipes away the falling tears;
Puts His arms of love around her,
Saying, "Child be of good cheer;
Though your sins may be as scarlet,
I will make them like as wool;
Though they may be red like crimson,
I will make them white as snow."

2. She has sinned and she must suffer,
    says the world so hard and cold,

She's no soul that she possesses, we
     have bought it with our gold;
Do not lend a hand to save her, cast
     her out and let her go.
From her heart will wring a wail of
     bitter woe.
See, there she stands beside the river,
Dark waters rolling at her feet, invites
     her to their cold embrace.
"If they only would forgive me, if
     they'd only let me try,
But the world has closed its door and
     I must die."

3. Round the corner comes the Army,
     oh, how sweet the timbrels sound !
"Bless you, Captain, hurry quickly,
     here's a jewel for your crown;"
Right wheel, soldiers, form a circle;
     you are on the right street now;
Sing a song of Jesus saves—He saves
     me now.
She hears the song, she stops to listen,
Another verse, she's drawing near; the
     Captain takes her by the hand,
"Will He save me? I will trust Him—
     Lord, remember not the past."
Joy in Heaven, Christ has conquered,
     saved at last.

151

Come to the Saviour.

1. Come to the Saviour, come to the
     Saviour,
Thou sin-stricken offspring of man;
He left His throne above
   To reveal His wondrous love,
And to open a fountain for sin.

I do believe it! I do believe it!
   I'm saved through the blood of the
     Lamb;
My happy soul is free, for the Lord
     has pardoned me,
   Hallelujah to Jesus' name !

2. Why dost thou linger? Why dost
     thou linger?
Oh, when wilt thou haste to be saved?
   Thy time is flying fast,
   And thy day will soon be past;
Oh, arouse thee, and come and be
     saved !

3. Pardon is offered, pardon is offered,
A pardon full, present and free;
   Thy mighty debt was paid
   When on Calvary Jesus died
To atone for a rebel like thee.

4. Plunge in the fountain, plunge in
     the fountain,
The fountain which cleanses the soul;
   'Tis cleansing far and near,   -
   And its streams are flowing here,
Oh, believe it, and thou art made
     whole !

152

Whiter Than the Snow.

Tune—"Whiter than the Snow." B. J.
                         12.

1. Tell me what to do to be pure
   In the sight of All-seeing Eyes !
Tell me is there no thorough cure,
   No escape from sins I despise?
Tell me, can I never be free
   From terrible bondage within?
Is there no deliverance for me,
   Must I always struggle with sin?

CHORUS.

   Whiter than the snow,
Wash me in the blood of the Lamb,
   And I shall be whiter than snow.

2. Will my Saviour only pass by?
   Only show me how faulty I've
     been?
Will He not attend to my cry?
   Can I not this moment be clean?
Blessed Lord, almighty to heal,
   I know that Thy power cannot fail;
Here and now I know—yes, I feel,
   The prayer of my heart does pre-
     vail.

153

Room at the Cross.

G Flat.

1. There is room at the cross, will
     you bring, wand'rer,
   Your heart by sin's night made so
     black?
Weary, footsore, through treading
     rough paths, wand'rer,
There's light only on Calvary's track.

It shines from the cross, will you look, wand'rer.
To Him who has suffered for you?
There is life, there is joy, there is hope, wand'rer,
There is room at the cross now for you.

CHORUS.

There is room at the cross for you now, wand'rer.
There is room at the cross for you now;
There is life, there is joy, there is hope, wand'rer,
There is room at the cross for you now.

2. Every day brings you nearer to your doom, wand'rer,
Just now on the verge you may be;
Just one step more may carry you down, wand'rer,
Into endless eternity.
Then lost! lost forever, no hope, wand'rer,
No hope, but despair, mercy gone;
Hear the voice that is pleading to-night, wand'rer,
There is room at the cross, will you come?

3. Every day makes it harder to break, wand'rer,
Away from the fleeting joys of earth;
But their pleasure will fade and decay, wand'rer,
In your life of joy there is dearth.
Each moment is drawing you near, wand'rer,
Will you at His cross come and bow?
There is life, there is joy, there is hope, wand'rer,
There is room at the cross for you now.

154

Take This Message to My Mother.

Tune—"Take This Letter to My Mother."

1. Take this message to my mother,
It will fill her heart with joy;
Tell her that her prayer is answered,
Christ has saved her wandering boy.

Tho' through sin from home I've wandered,
And I almost broke her heart.
Tell her to be glad and cheerful,
Never from the Lord I'll part.

CHORUS.

Take this message to my mother,
It will fill her heart with joy;
Tell her that her prayer is answered,
Christ has saved her wandering boy.

2. When I from my mother parted
How her heart did ache with pain,
When she said, "Good-bye, God bless you!
We may never meet again;
Oh, my boy, just look to Jesus,
What a Friend He is to all;
Only trust Him, He will save you,
Can't you hear His sweet voice call?"

155

I am Trusting, Lord, in Thee.

Tune—"I Am Coming to the Cross."
Key, E Flat."

1. I am coming to the Cross,
I am poor and weak and blind,
I am counting all but dross,
I shall full salvation find.

CHORUS.

I am trusting, Lord, in Thee,
Blessed Lamb of Calvary;
Humbly at Thy Cross I bow,
Jesus saves me, saves me now.

2. Long my heart has sighed for Thee,
Long has evil reigned within;
Jesus sweetly speaks to me:
"I will cleanse you from all sin."

3. Here I give my all to Thee,
Friends and time and earthly store.
Soul and body Thine to be,
Wholly Thine for evermore.

4. In the promises, I trust,
Now I feel the blood applied;
I am prostrate in the dust,
I with Christ am crucified.

5. Jesus comes, He fills my soul,
Perfected in love I am;
I am every whit made whole,
Glory, glory to the Lamb.

156

Lord, Jesus, I Long to be Perfectly Whole.

Tune—"Whiter Than Snow." G. Flat.

1. Lord Jesus, I long to be perfectly
   whole,
I want Thee forever to live in my soul;
Break down every idol, cast out every
   foe,
Now wash me and I shall be whiter
   than snow.

CHORUS.

Whiter than snow; yes, whiter than
   snow;
Now wash me and I shall be whiter
   than snow.

2. Lord Jesus, let nothing unholy remain,
Apply Thine own blood and remove
   every stain;
To get this blest washing I all things
   forego,
Now wash me and I shall be whiter
   than snow.

3. Lord Jesus, come down from Thy
   Throne in the skies,
And help me to make a complete sacri-
   fice;
I give up myself and whatever I know,
Now wash me and I shall be whiter
   than snow.

4. Lord Jesus, Thou seest I patiently
   wait,
Come now and within me a new heart
   create;
To those who have sought Thee Thou
   never saidst "No,"
Now wash me and I shall be whiter
   than snow.

5. Lord Jesus, for this I most humbly
   entreat,
I wait, blessed Lord, at Thy crucified
   feet;
By faith, for my cleansing, I see Thy
   blood flow,
Now wash me and I shall be whiter
   than snow.

157

I am Trusting in the Pilot.

A Flat.

I am sailing on an ocean wide and
   deep,
Where the storms of time around me
   constant sweep;
And the wrecks that float around me
   as I glide,
Onward go without a Saviour's hand
   to guide;
While my bark is borne along the
   sweeping tide,
   I am trusting in the Pilot safe and
   sure;
Storms may rage and yet no harm can
   e'er betide,
   I am trusting in the Pilot safe and
   sure.

CHORUS.

I am trusting in the Pilot, trusting in
   the Pilot,
Trusting in the Pilot safe and sure.
(Repeat.)

2. On the shore my loved ones wait
   and watch for me,
They have passed in safety o'er the
   troubled sea;
And the wind that whips the waters
   wild to foam,
Only drives my speeding vessel nearer
   home.
Soon my bark will land me safe on
   Heaven's shore,
   I am trusting in the Pilot safe and
   sure;
I shall meet my friends to part with
   them no more,
   I am trusting in the Pilot safe and
   sure.

3. Oh, poor soul that's tossed about
   with wind and wave!
Though you struggle on and many
   dangers brave;
Yet, when time shall end, my brother,
   do you think
Will you safely sail or will your vessel
   sink?
Jesus Christ is near to lend a helping
   hand,
   Will you trust Him for your Pilot
   safe and sure?

He will pilot you safe into Heaven's
    land
    If you'll trust Him for your Pilot
    safe and sure.

158

There's Mercy Still for Thee.

1. Oh, wanderer, knowing not the
    smile
Of Jesus' lovely face,
In darkness living all the while,
    Rejecting offered grace:
To thee Jehovah's voice doth sound,
    Thy soul He waits to free;
Thy Saviour hath a ransom found,
    There's mercy still for thee!

CHORUS.

There's mercy still for thee!
There's mercy still for thee!
    Poor, trembling soul,
    He'll make thee whole,
There's mercy still for thee!

2. Long in the darkness thou hast
    strayed
    Away from joy and peace:
Thou hast these worldly pleasures
    tried,
    But found them soon to cease.
Without one lingering ray of hope,
    In anguish thou may'st be;
Oh, listen to the joyful sound,
    There's mercy still for thee!

3. For thee, though sunk in deep
    despair,
    Thy Saviour's blood was shed;
He for thy sin was as a lamb
    To cruel slaughter led.
That thou may'st find, poor sin-sick
    soul,
    A pardon full and free;
What boundless grace, what wondrous
    love,
    There's mercy still for thee!

4. Though sins of years rise mountains
    high,
    And would thy hopes destroy,
Thy Saviour's blood can wash away
    The stains and bring thee joy.
Now lift thy heart in earnest prayer,
    To Him for safety flee;
While still the angels chant the strain,
    There's mercy still for thee!

159

Be in Time.

Tune—"Meet Me There."

D Flat.

1. Life at best is very brief,
Like the falling of a leaf,
Like the binding of a sheaf—
    Be in time!
Fleeting days are telling fast
That the die will soon be cast,
And the fatal line be past—
    Be in time!

CHORUS.

Be in time, be in time,
While the voice of Jesus calls you,
    Be in time!
If in sin you longer wait,
You will find an open gate,
But your sad cry be "Too late!"
    Be in time!

2. Fairest flowers soon decay.
Youth and beauty pass away;
Oh, you have not long to stay!
    Be in time!
While the Spirit bids you come,
Sinner, do not longer roam,
Lest you seal your hopeless doom,
    Be in time!

3. Time is gliding swiftly by,
Death and judgment draweth nigh.
To the arms of Jesus fly—
    Be in time!
Oh, I pray you count the cost
Ere the fatal line be crossed,
And your soul in Hell be lost!
    Be in time!

160

My Wandering Boy.

A Flat.

1. Out in the cold world and far away
    from home,
Some mother's boy is wandering all
    alone;
No one to guide him or keep his foot-
    steps right,
Some mother's boy is homeless to-
    night.
Search till you find him and bring
    him back to me,
Far, far away, wherever he may be,

Tell him his mother, with faded cheeks
   and hair,
At the old home is waiting for him
   there.

CHORUS.

Bring back my boy, my wandering boy,
There is no other left to give me joy;
Tell him his mother, with faded cheeks
   and hair,
At the old home is waiting him there.

2. Oh, could I see him and press him
   to my breast,
Gladly I'd close my eyes and be at rest!
There's no other left to bring me joy,
Bring back to me my wandering boy;
Well I remember the parting words he
   said,
"We'll meet up there where no fare-
   wells are said;
There'll be no good-byes in that bright
   world so fair,
When done with life, I'll meet you up
   there."

3. Out in the hall there stands a vacant
   chair,
Yonder the shoes that he once used to
   wear;
Empty the cradle that he once loved
   so well;
Oh, how I love him no one can tell!
Could I forget him or cease to hold
   him dear?
Still he's my boy as when he was here,
Though he has wandered in darkness
   and sin,
Bring him to me, I will welcome him
   in.

161

What a Gathering That Will Be!

*(By permission of Messrs. Eaton and
Mains.)*

1. At the sounding of the trumpet,
   when the saints are gather'd
   home,
  We will greet each other by the
   crystal sea;
With the friends and all the loved
   ones there awaiting us to come,
  What a gathering of the faithful
   that will be!

CHORUS.

What a gath'ring, gath'ring,
  At the sounding of the glorious
   jubilee!
What a gath'ring, gath'ring,
  What a gath'ring of the faithful
   that will be!

2. When the angel of the Lord proclaims that time shall be no
   more,
We shall gather, and the saved and
   ransom'd see,
Then to meet again together on the
   bright, celestial shore,
  What a gath'ring of the faithful that
   will be!

3. At the great and final judgment,
   when the hidden comes to light,
  When the Lord in all His glory we
   shall see,
At the bidding of our Saviour, "Come
   ye blessed, to My right,"
  What a gath'ring of the faithful that
   will be!

4. When the golden harps are sounding, and the angel bands pro-
   claim
  In triumphant strains the glorious
   jubilee,
Then to meet and join to sing the
   song of Moses and the Lamb,
  What a gath'ring of the faithful that
   will be!

162

Oh, Turn Ye!

Tune—"Oh, Turn Ye." B. J., 86. S.
   M., I., 160. 11s.

1. My Jesus, I love Thee, I know
   Thou art mine;
For Thee all the pleasures of sin I
   resign;
My gracious Redeemer, my Saviour
   art Thou,
If ever I loved Thee, my Jesus, 'tis
   now.

2. I love Thee because Thou hast first
   loved me,
And purchased my pardon when nailed
   to the tree;

I love Thee for wearing the thorns on
  Thy brow:
If ever I loved Thee, my Jesus, 'tis
  now.

3. I will love Thee in life, I will love
  Thee in death,
And praise Thee as long as Thou
  lendest me breath:
And say when the death-dew lies cold
  on my brow,
"If ever I loved Thee, my Jesus, 'tis
  now."

4. In mansions of glory and endless
  delight,
I'll ever adore Thee and dwell in Thy
  sight:
I'll sing with the glittering crown on
  my brow,
"If ever I loved Thee, my Jesus, 'tis
  now."

163

Oh, Say Will You Take Up Your Cross?

1. You have oft heard the call to
  surrender:
    God's Spirit with you oft has
      striven;
Now again at your heart He is speak-
  ing,
    And another blessed offer is given.

CHORUS.

Oh, say will you take up your cross?
Oh, say will you take up your cross?
The Saviour is waiting your answer!
Oh, say will you take up your cross?

2. His voice you have long disre-
  garded,
    Unheeded He's knocked at your
      door:
Sinner, now open wide to the Saviour,
    Lest He leave thee to knock ever-
      more.

3. There's a time coming on when
  you'll want Him
    To bear you safe over death's
      stream;
Then be wise and in time seek His
  favor,
    And just now, while He knocks, let
      Him in.

4. When He comes as a bridegroom
  at midnight,
    No time to prepare you will find;

Then you'll knock but in vain for ad-
  mittance,
    He will leave you in darkness be-
      hind.

164

He's Just The Same To-day.

1. When Moses and his people from
  Egypt's land did flee,
Their enemies behind them and in
  front of them the sea,
God raised the water like a wall and
  opened up their way,
And the God that lived in Moses' time
  is just the same to-day.

2. When Daniel, faithful to his God,
  would not bow down to men,
And by God's enemies were hurled
  into the lion's den,
God shut the lions' mouths we read
  and robbed them of their prey,
And the God that lived in Daniel's time
  is just the same to-day.

3. When David and Goliath met, the
  wrong against the right,
The giant armed with human power,
  and David with God's might,
God's power, with David's sling and
  stone the giant low did lay,
And the God that lived in David's time
  is just the same to-day.

4. When Paul and Silas were in jail
  their feet fast in the stocks,
God sent a mighty earthquake down
  and brake the prison locks;
He set both Paul and Silas free; He
  made the jailor pray,
And the God that lived in St. Paul's
  time is just the same to-day.

5. When Jonah disobeyed his God,
  and was swallowed by the whale,
The guilt and anguish that he bore no
  human tongue can tell;
God helped him make dry land again
  when willing to obey,
And the God that lived in Jonah's time
  is just the same to-day.

6. When Pentecost had fully come
  and fire from Heaven did fall,
Like a mighty wind the Holy Ghost
  baptized them one and all;
Three thousand got converted, and
  were soldiers right away,
And the God that lived at Pentecost
  is just the same to-day.

Salvation Choruses.

Key Bb.

There is mercy in Jesus.
Come away, come away.
Oh, the prodigal's coming home.
Born again, born again.
There's mercy still for thee.
Boundless love beyond degree.
Will your lamps be trimmed and
burning?
While the light from Heaven is fall-
ing.
Turn to the Lord and seek salvation.
Are you coming home?
Jesus died for you.
Oh, seek that beautiful stream.
Shall we meet beyond the river?
Who'll be the next to follow Jesus?
Come home, come home.
Prepare me, prepare me, Lord.
Only Jesus will I know.

Key Ah.

At the cross.
Down at the cross, down at the cross.
The wounds of Christ are open.
God is near thee, tell thy story.
Come with thy sin.
On the banks of the beautiful river.
Life's morn will soon be waning.
We shall walk through the valley.
Come to Jesus.
Turn to the Lord and seek salvation.
Say, poor sinner, wouldn't you like to
go?
Come to Jesus, come to Jesus just
now.
Behold Me standing at the door.
Eternity, eternity, where will you
spend eternity?
Oh, Lamb of God, I come.

Key G.

Take all my sins away.
Oh, no, nothing do I bring.
When the mighty, mighty, mighty
trump sounds.
Safe in the arms of Jesus.
Oh, remember Calvary!
There are angels hovering round.
Almost persuaded.
Oh, say, shall we meet you all there?
I am coming to the cross.
For you I am praying.
Then open and let the Master in.
My Lord what a mourning!

What can wash away my sins?
He is waiting.
Hark, hear the Saviour knocking!
(Tune—"Scatter seeds.")
For Jesus, my Saviour, will welcome
sinners home.
Listen to her pleading, "Wandering
boy, come home!"

Key F.

Oh, the drunkard may come.
For the conquering Saviour.
Oh, take me as I am!
Ere the sun, ere the sun goes down.
All the world can ne'er console thee.
Work for the night is coming.
Dear Jesus, on Calvary.
While the heavenly music.
The precious blood of Jesus it washes
white as snow.
Why not to-night?
Jesus is calling.
Oh, Saviour, I am coming!
Steal away to Jesus.
Hasten home quickly. Jesus will meet
thee.

Key Eb.

You are drifting to your doom.
Oh, yes, there's salvation for you!
Oh, touch the hem of His garment.
Haste away to Jesus.
Knocking, knocking, who is there?
I am coming, Lord. (Tune—"Jesus
paid it all.")
For the Lion of Judah.

Key C.

Jesus now is passing by.
You never can tell when the Lord will
call you.
Death is coming, coming, coming.
Oh, Calvary's stream is flowing.
Prepare me, prepare me, Lord.
Of Calvary, of Calvary.
Ask the Saviour to help you.
Tell me the old, old story.
Come, sinner, will you meet us on
Canaan's peaceful shore?
Sown in the darkness and sown in the
light.

Key D.

I'm trusting, I'm trusting; at the cross
of Christ I bow.

Holiness Choruses.

Key G.

Oh, it comes o'er my soul like a wave.
Over me, over me it is flowing.
Dear Jesus is the One I love.
No, no, no, no, I count no sacrifice too
  dear.
Perfect peace I enjoy.
The cross now covers my sins.
I am glad there is cleansing in the
  blood.
Beautiful cross, wonderful cross.
I will follow the Lamb.
That means me.
Oh, yes, there's victory in Jesus for
  me.
He is bringing to His fold.
Fill me now.
Then scatter seeds of kindness.
Have faith in God.

Key Ab.

Come, oh, come, Great Spirit, come.
Give me a heart like Thine.
I'll follow Thee, of life the giver.
Pour Thy Spirit.
I have a Saviour who's mighty to
  keep.
Only Jesus will I know.
The cleansing stream I see, I see.
Glory, glory, hallelujah! I have given
  my all to God.
Keep on believing, Jesus is near.
Reign, oh, reign, my Saviour.
It's rolling in, it's rolling in.
I'm believing and receiving.
It was on the cross He shed His blood.
He pardoned a rebel like me.
The cross now covers my sins.
'Tis the very same power.
I need Thee every hour.
Whiter than snow.
Oh, how I love Jesus!
Where He leads I will follow.
For the cross I am ready. (Tune—
  "Trim your lamps and be
  ready.")
To the uttermost He saves.
It's all I want—a lot more faith.

Key F.

All I have I am bringing to Thee.
At Thy feet I fall.
Thine, Thine, I will be Thine.
All my heart I give Thee.

Oh, the blood, to me so dear.
Oh, 'tis coming! Oh, 'tis coming!
Oh, the blood of Jesus cleanses white
  as snow.
Oh, that's the place!
Oh, the Lamb, the bleeding Lamb!
Rolled away.
I do believe it! I do believe it!
Oh, it was love, 'twas wondrous love.
Down at the fountain, flowing so free.
Oh, what a Redeemer!
Oh, the waters of Jordan may roll.
Jesus has redeemed me.
I dare, Lord; I dare, Lord; I dare do
  all for Thee.
In the cross.
He's the Lily of the Valley, oh, my
  Lord.
Now it comes o'er my soul like a wave.
Fire descending, descending, descend-
  ing. (Tune—"Jesus is call-
  ing.")
I'll live for Him who died for me."

Key Eb.

Living beneath the shade of the cross.
Saviour, my all I surrender.
Oh, glory to His name!
I will follow Thee, my Saviour.
Ever Thine, Thine alone.
Power, power, power divine.
Oh, the peace my Saviour gives.
Yes, He gave me peace and pardon.
I have loved and lived with Jesus.
There's a laying down of crosses.
My sins, my sins, are under the blood.
Anywhere with Jesus.
My all is on the altar.
I'm claiming, I'm claiming.
No, never; no, never alone.

Key C.

Keep me unspotted from sin, dear
  Saviour.
Down at the Saviour's feet.
I will not let Thee go.
I'll cling closer to Jesus.
Thou art a mighty Saviour.
I think of all His sorrow.
Draw me nearer, nearer, nearer,
  blessed Lord.
God is love, I know, I feel.
Fall on me.
Touch me! Touch me. (Tune—
  "Come home.".)

Key Bb.

Saviour, dear Saviour, draw nearer.
Thou hast the power to heal me.
The precious blood is flowing o'er my heart.
My Lord, oh, let the waves of Thy crimson sea.
I bring my all to Thee, dear Jesus.
My heart is now whiter than snow.
Oh, speak while before Thee I pray.
Speak, Saviour, speak.
Jesus is strong to deliver.

Grace there is my every debt to pay.
A wonderful Saviour is Jesus.
Oh, for the hallowing flame.
'Tis while in faith I'm kneeling.
Wonderful, wonderful, wonderful love.
Oh, send another Pentecost!
Power, power, power divine.
My heart's door wide I'm swinging.
Rock of Ages, cleft for me.
Rescue the perishing.
To Thy cross I come, Lord.

Rejoicing and Victory Choruses.

Key Ab.

No, we never, never, never will give in!
When the road we tread is rough.
I believe we shall win.
Oh, I am a soldier. Glory to God!
March on, march on, we bring the jubilee.
With the conquering Son of God.
We will march through the world with the fire and the blood.
Then awake, then awake.
No retreating, Hell defeating.
Bright crowns there are.
At the end of our journey.
When the trumpet sounds.
That means me.
I'm washed in the blood of the Lamb.
Blessedly saved, saved by the blood.
So we'll stand the storm.
Saved and kept by the grace of God.
Glory to God! I'm at the fountain drinking.
I'm going to spend eternity singing around the throne.
Salvation is the best thing in the world.
Let the blessed sunshine in.
My home is in Heaven.
'Tis well with the righteous, well.
My sins rose as high as a mountain.

Key F.

We're the Army that shall conquer.
Steadily forward march.
Oh, the crowning day is coming. Hallelujah!
The yellow, red and blue shall fly.

And above the rest this note shall swell.
Oh, salvation, full and free!
I love Jesus. Hallelujah!
Away over Jordan.
He arose from the dead.
I'm the child of a King.
On, on, no evil befalling me. (Tune—"Oh, dear, what can the matter be?")

Key Eb.

We shall conquer all through the blood of Jesus.
Never say die.
Marching along, we are marching along.
Keep waving, keep waving, keep every flag unfurled.

Key C.

We'll all shout Hallelujah!
Marching on, marching on.
Fighting, fighting on the narrow way.
I'll stand for Christ alone.
There's no one like Jesus can cheer me to-day.
Oh, I'm climbing up the golden stair to glory.
Joy, joy, wonderful joy.
Down where the living waters flow.
The heavenly gales are blowing.
Glory, glory, hallelujah!
My beautiful home.
Joy bells, joy bells, never cease ringing.
If the cross we boldly bear.
So we'll lift up the banner.

He's the Lily of the Valley. (Tune—
   "Just tell my dear old mother."
Lord, keep the fire burning.

Key G.

Oh, I'm glad I'm ready.
A never failing friend.
He's the Lily of the Valley.
Let us walk in the light.
Hallelujah! Send the glory.
Happy day! Happy day!
All the way long it is Jesus.
There is sweet rest in Heaven.
Hallelujah! 'tis done!
So we'll roll the old chariot along.
He gave me joy.
Praise God, I'm saved!
Jesus, Jesus, precious and sweet.
The war, the war, the Salvation War.

Key D.

I am redeemed.
Living beneath the shade of the cross.

Key Bb.

Fully trusting in the battle's fray.
The day of victory's coming.
I'll gird on the armor.
'Twas a happy day and no mistake.
The light of the world is Jesus.
There is sunlight, blessed sunlight.
Gone is my burden.
We'll cross the river of Jordan.
This is where you'll find us.

Key Db.

God be with you till we meet again.

SINGING SALVATION INTO SINNERS SOULS

INDEX.

Titles in Italics. First lines in Roman.

INDEX.

INDEX.